Lives in Cricket: No

C.P.Lewis
The Champion Cricketer of South Wales

Bob Harragan and Andrew Hignell

With a foreword by Ian Hunt

First published in Great Britain by
Association of Cricket Statisticians and Historians
Cardiff CF11 9XR
© ACS, 2009

British Library Cataloguing-in-Publication Data.
A catalogue record for this book is available from the British
Library.

ISBN: 978 1 905138 78 4
Typeset by Limlow Books

Contents

Foreword
By Ian Hunt
Warden of Llandovery College

I am delighted to write this foreword, celebrating the life and achievements of C.P.Lewis, one of the most famous *alumni* from Llandovery College, and a man whose achievements over a hundred years ago are still revered, and celebrated, in the College today.

Sport played a massive part of C.P.Lewis' life and, as someone who has spent many years in teaching, I am acutely aware of the benefits that participation in healthy recreation can play in a young person's development, as well as their later life on leaving school or university. C.P.Lewis may have been involved in the sporting life of Llandovery College back in the 1870s and 1880s, but even now in the twenty-first century, the benefits of taking part in sport, playing for a team, and obeying rules and regulations are still key ingredients in the wider education of our young people, and are amongst the core values at Llandovery College today.

As the authors have portrayed in this fascinating account, C.P.Lewis was able play both rugby and cricket at a very high standard, and this is perhaps the only major difference with Wales' leading sportsmen and women today. But here at Llandovery College we still value the essence of being a good all-rounder, displaying skills in a number of areas and, where possible, combining excellence in the classroom with excellence on the sports field.

At a time when there is plenty of debate at government level about the content of a school's curriculum, and the role of subjects such as History and Physical Education, this booklet is an apt reminder that we can learn important lessons from the past, and that not all history is bunk!

Indeed, in the year when Test cricket has come to Wales, with Glamorgan's headquarters in Cardiff hosting an Ashes Test, we owe it to our younger generation to give them a good, and proper, grounding in these key skills, and ensuring that those inspired by watching the English and Australian cricketers this summer can have an opportunity to emulate the feats of C.P.Lewis – a great Welsh sportsman and a truly great Llandoverian.

Llandovery
July, 2009

Introduction

English cricket historians have, quite rightly, made much of the likes of William Clarke, the Lillywhites and Charles Alcock in promoting and administering cricket and other games in the second half of the nineteenth century. Until now, little has been written about the prominent early figures in the development of sport in Wales, but similar plaudits are long overdue to Charles Prytherch Lewis who, like Alcock, was a leading figure in the development of winter and summer games.

Not only was he a major force in the early development of rugby in Wales – and the earliest-born Welsh rugby international – C.P.Lewis was a key mover and shaker in the evolution of regional and county cricket in the Principality during the second half of the nineteenth century, laying the foundations upon which the Glamorgan County Cricket Club was formed in July 1888.

Lewis played cricket for the South Wales Cricket Club and for Oxford University; rugby for Wales; and, as if this was not enough, he also won an athletics half-Blue. Besides being one of the people who played a leading role in the early years of the Welsh Rugby Union during the 1880s, he was perhaps the finest cricketer in the Principality during that era – a time when several key changes took place to the sporting landscape of Wales, with the development of thriving rugby and cricket clubs, a national rugby team, successful regional cricket teams, and embryonic county elevens. It was a measure of Lewis' sporting eminence that he played a leading role in all of these developments.

As far as cricket is concerned, he played at a time when important changes were taking place to the game throughout England, and he was in his prime at the time of the beginnings of the modern County Championship and the tentative, as yet unnamed, beginnings of Test cricket. Indeed he might have been one of the earliest Test cricketers if he had acted on an apparent invitation to join the 1878/79 Gentlemen's tour of Australia, originally to be led by I.D. ('Donny') Walker of Southgate in Middlesex – although as the fiery fast bowler, his presence might have scotched the engagements of the professionals Emmett and Ulyett, and early statisticians may have been less willing to class their match against Australia as a Test.

He was over six feet tall – big for that period – and, at his peak, weighed 12st 6lb, though his waistband expanded with age, particularly when he gave up rugby and his fast bowling started to fade. As a right-arm bowler, Lewis was described by contemporaries as 'round-hand fast', and from the number of clean-bowled victims in his bag he seems to have been particularly accurate. The green *Lillywhite* annual also once recorded of him: 'C.P.Lewis has a low slinging delivery when bowling, but the ball gets up quick from the pitch, and as his direction is fairly accurate, he sometimes has success. A hard hitter.'

Lewis had been a fairly successful bowler with Oxford University in 1876 taking, in five first-class matches, 17 wickets at 29 runs apiece. His invitation to join the tour of Australia does not seem to be documented at the time, surfacing years later in his obituary notice, so we cannot judge how accurate the claim was, or whether it was a boastful comment which he had made in his later years.

Tradition has it that he was also asked to play against the Australians for a Gentlemen of England side in 1878 or 1880, but was unable to do so: he did, though, play against them for XVIII of South Wales on the first of these tours. He played several times for M.C.C. against various teams – he eventually became of member of the premier English club in 1886 – but it seems he was not much of a joiner-in at high-level sport in England. Indeed, on coming down from Oxford in 1876, he accepted an offer to return to teach at his *alma mater*, Llandovery College and, in keeping with the custom at that time, played both cricket and rugby alongside his pupils for the College side.

With some promising talent emerging in the Llandovery XI, it was no surprise that the schoolboys, together with a gleeful C.P.Lewis, swept aside the leading adult Welsh clubs and in 1881 won the South Wales Challenge Cup – the premier competition at the time which ran alongside the almost identical South Wales Rugby Football Challenge Cup, with nearly equal prestige and rowdy crowds. During his time teaching at Llandovery, Lewis also won five Welsh rugby caps, and led the side in three of his international appearances in the early 1880s. Over a dozen of his charges at the College also went on to win Welsh rugby caps.

His senior cricket during the late nineteenth century was as vice-captain – very often the playing captain – of the South Wales Cricket Club on its annual 'London' tour, which a decade before Lewis' advent had introduced W.G.Grace to big cricket. When this socially exclusive team split up 'to form county sides' his teammates and neighbours waited more than a dozen years while urging him to set in train a Carmarthenshire side to equal the improving Glamorgan and Monmouthshire teams with their Minor County ambitions. In the end, a younger generation took things into their own hands. By then, Lewis, busy in his legal practice, had virtually retired, but he did come back to lend a badly needed hand to Carmarthenshire's struggling Minor Counties side during the early 1900s.

He was, by this time, well into his fifties – and not, judging by his photographs, a particularly fit man. Instead, he was heavily built, well-dined, and looking as if he might suffer from gout or other problems associated with gentlemen of that age. But he played, and often captained Carmarthenshire sides as they tried – sadly, in vain – to establish themselves as a Minor County.

It was far from the glories of his youthful years. The avuncular figure of the early twentieth century was very different from the images of his youthful years when a 'team photograph' of the solidly staid and scholarly masters at Llandovery College included Lewis, lounging against a wall, schoolmaster's robes ill-fitting and out of place on what is clearly a young man not used to standing still. That picture, seen in Chapter Five, shows his hair windblown and unruly, different, even in a time of big whiskers and sideburns.

When teaching at Llandovery, C.P. was a well-liked member of the College's community: in fact, he could hardly be anything less, given his sporting prowess and standing as a Welsh rugby international of some repute. He ran Trafalgar House – one of the boarding houses used by the College to house the adolescent boys – and no doubt C.P. regaled his impressionable charges with tales of derring-do on the sports fields of Wales and England. In later life, he continued to have a fund of stories, some greatly embellished, which he told, sometimes with cheerful exaggeration, to his friends and acquaintances in the Llandovery area after he had changed careers during the early 1880s to become a solicitor in the old droving town at the foot of Wales' central mountains.

9

Llandovery College when Lewis taught at the school.

His decision to leave Llandovery College in 1883 – at a time when he was leading the Welsh rugby team and playing cricket for the South Wales club – is one of several quite interesting dimensions to his adult life, and sports historians have often wondered what his motives were. Another question is: 'Why did Lewis not involve himself with the Glamorgan county club when it was formed in 1888?' This was just a couple of years after the winding up of the South Wales C.C. for whom he had been a leading figure, with a wide range of contacts. His county cricket until then had been for Breconshire, just a few miles to the north-east of Llandovery, or for Carmarthenshire. Either or even both of these county sides might have contributed to the 'All Wales' side which Glamorgan eventually became in the twentieth century, with the south-east of Wales holding the commercial and political power for a county club to last and thrive.

Indeed, there were few people in sporting circles in Wales, and beyond, in the 1880s who had not heard of C.P.Lewis, who by then was still a bachelor in his mid-thirties, and seemingly a fine catch for a young lady. Yet it was not until 1892, when back in Llandovery and in line to be the town's Mayor, that C.P. got married – at the age of 39 – to a lady eight years his senior.

This book seeks to find answers to some of these questions about the life and times of C.P.Lewis, and attempts to set the record straight about one of the earliest leading cricketers and sporting personalities in Wales, paying tribute to his many outstanding and varied achievements.

Chapter One

School Days in Llandovery, Swansea and Gloucester

Charles Prytherch Lewis was born on 20 August 1853 at Llwyn Celyn, just outside the small town of Llangadog in rural Carmarthenshire, about 20 miles north of Swansea and 40 miles north-west of Cardiff. The town lies in the Tywi Valley, in the lee of Brynamman Mountain, from the top of which, it used to be said that you could see five counties. The house where he was born is referred to in some sources as being at Llanwrda, a village about two miles north of Llangadog: in reality, it is part way between the two settlements. His uncle, the Rev David Price Lewis, J.P., was the first to live in the house. He died a bachelor in 1861, when it passed to C.P.'s father, Frederick, who was listed in the 1851 and 1861 censuses as a 'landed proprietor'. The Lewises were a county family of sufficient significance for genealogists to have traced them back several centuries. In the 1881 census the name, though relatively rare in England, was common throughout Wales, but was

Llwyn Celyn, near Llangadog, C.P.'s early home.

most readily found in West Glamorgan and the counties of Brecon, Cardigan, Carmarthen and Pembroke. The name means offspring of 'Llewi', itself short for Llewellyn, which in its turn refers back to Llewellyn, the famous name of the last independent Prince of Wales.

C.P. was the fifth of seven children born to Frederick and his wife, Anna Letitia, née Price. He had two older brothers; Frederick William, who became a doctor and served as Medical Officer of Health for Llandovery; and David Jones, who subsequently became a barrister. He had a younger brother, Arthur Middleton, who became a stockbroker and lived in later life in Surbiton in Surrey. C.P. also had two older sisters – Anna and Mary Agnes – plus a younger sister, Emily Louisa, and the Lewis family lived, comfortably it would seem, at Llwyn Celyn with a governess, a groom and five other servants. Another measure of their decent situation was that Frederick and his wife could afford to pay the full tuition and boarding fees for all of their boys at Llandovery College, in the town of that name five miles further up the Tywi valley from Llangadog.

The College had been endowed by Thomas Phillips, a London-born but Radnorshire-bred gentleman who spent thirty years in India, before retiring to London and becoming important in the Royal College of Surgeons. For a while in younger life, he had been a surgeon's apprentice in Hay-on-Wye, near the Welsh border, about thirty miles from Llandovery. When he wanted to promote educational links between Welsh speakers and the church, he offered to fund a professorship in Welsh at the theological college of St. David's, Lampeter. However, his offer was oddly and rudely rebuffed by the college authorities and so, Kerry Packer-like, Phillips decided to go it alone in Llandovery, a drovers' town where herds of Welsh cows and flocks of sheep rested as they were driven from the mountain pastures to the markets of London. It was a most apt location for his Welsh Collegiate Institute, because it was a stop on the stagecoach ride of the Bishop of St. David's from his palace at Abergwili, outside Carmarthen, to London, and his support was thought crucial. Llandovery – in its pure Welsh form it translates as 'The Church amongst the Waters' – stands at the confluence of three rivers – the Tywi, the great salmon river that runs from the mountains of mid-Wales through Carmarthenshire to the sea, splitting west Wales in half, with the smaller Bran and

Gwydderug. It was the 'pleasantest little town' according to the Victorian gentleman author, George Borrow, writing in 1862.

C.P's county, Carmarthenshire, on an eighteenth-century map, showing many of the places figuring in his story, with variant spellings. In spite of several local government reorganisations, the county still has similar administrative boundaries.

The Institute was opened in 1848, and there is evidence of early interest in cricket as its library was said to contain an 1830 book titled '*Handbook of Cricket*'. (This is more likely the 1838 *Cricketer's Hand Book* 'containing the origin of the game, remarks on recent alterations, directions for bowling, striking, and placing the players, and the laws as altered by the M.C.C.', unless we have uncovered evidence for an earlier edition than previously recorded.) It was not until Lewis attended the school in the 1860s that its cricket developed into a substantial activity. By then the railway had arrived in the town, within three years bringing easier links to Cardiff, south-west England and the English midlands, though change appears to have been slow and there was little impact on the college and its scholars for many years. Cricket in

Llandovery is first mentioned by Arthur Haygarth in *Scores and Biographies* in September 1873, which gives the score of a match between Llandovery College and Christ College, Brecon. Haygarth says he was putting the game in 'as a curiosity', with Brecon being all out for nine. 'It contains no names of note,' he says. Lewis batted at three but was out for a duck, but took five lower-order wickets – four of them bowled and one lbw – before steering his side to victory with 12 not out.

This annual contest, which had started in 1872, was between the two leading public schools in South Wales, and later came to be regarded as the Eton *v* Harrow match of Wales. Cricket was first played at Llandovery College seven years before. Like many other schools in Wales at the time, the incorporation of rugby and cricket into the timetable at Llandovery stemmed from the appointment of a new member of staff at the school. In Llandovery's case this was an old boy of Cowbridge Grammar School, Rev Watkin Price Whittington, who had first recognized the benefits of healthy recreation whilst at school in Cowbridge, before studying Classics at Jesus College, Oxford.

Whittington's family hailed from the Neath area, and like a good 'muscular Christian',[1] he regularly kept wicket for the Cadoxton Club, who at the time were amongst the leading clubs in South Wales. He also played for the Glamorganshire side in 1869, before devoting his attention to teaching, at Llandovery and later at Ruthin School in North Wales where he served as Headmaster from 1881 until 1909.

He became Second Master at Llandovery in 1868, and for a while he inspired and nurtured the sporting talents of the young C.P., who had joined his elder brothers at the College in the mid 1860s. Lewis quickly made his mark in academic and sporting circles, and the arrival of Whittington helped to boost the youngster's abilities, especially on the rugby field. As Whittington later recalled: 'Coming as I did from Merchiston Castle – the best school in

---

[1] A term, perhaps derisive in original intent, used to describe a Victorian movement largely associated with the English authors Charles Kingsley and Thomas Hughes. Kingsley thought that 'games conduce not merely to physical but to moral health'. Hughes suggested that, particularly for men, it was 'a good thing to have strong and well-exercised bodies,' which should be 'used for the protection of the weak, the advancement of all righteous causes, and the subduing of the earth'. C.J.Bartlett has identified some 200 players who appeared in first-class cricket in the United Kingdom between 1850 and 1899 who were church ministers at the time or became one later, almost all of them Anglicans. These, and many others of lesser cricket talent, had a significant effect in schools and parishes throughout much of England and Wales.

Scotland for rugby football – once I found that the boys at Llandovery played a sort of Association football without definite rule, I introduced rugby and it thrived wonderfully. The boys quickly took to it, and rejoiced in it, and we never looked at Association football again. The masters of my time did all they could to foster a love of cricket and to create a good school XI, but cricket did not thrive like rugby football.'

Nevertheless, Lewis seems to have followed up much of the advice imparted by Whittington and put it to good practice, as in May 1868, when C.P. had a fine all-round game for the College – at the age of just fourteen – against Swansea Grammar School. He opened both the batting and bowling as the College won by an innings after dismissing the Swansea schoolboys for just 13 and 29. Batting first, the Llandovery team had made 89, with C.P., according to *The Cambrian*, 'making a well played score of 26 when he was bowled by Schenk.'

But the influence of Whittington on the adolescent Lewis was only very brief as the youngster suffered a series of tragic blows during the 1860s. The first had happened in the first week of June 1861, before C.P.'s days at the College, when his mother Anna died at the relatively early age of 44 as a result of heart failure caused, as outlined on her death certificate, by hypertrophic cardiomyopathy – a genetic disease in which the heart muscle thickens abnormally, often as the result of strenuous exercise, or as in Anna's case, multiple childbirth. However, it can also result in premature and sudden death, and the effect of his mother's abrupt passing can only be imagined, and the chance to play in various sports at the College, and to mix with the other sons of the local gentry, must have helped to take the eight-year-old's mind away from this domestic tragedy.

However, the harsh realities of Victorian life dealt C.P. another blow in early March 1866, when his father Frederick contracted a severe bout of bronchitis which resulted in his death on 15 March, at the age of 54. Together with the rest of the Lewis children who lived at Llwyn Celyn, they became the charges of their uncle, Rev Charles Prytherch Williams who had been vicar of Llanddewi and curate of Port Eynon, on the Gower peninsula, before focussing his efforts on running a school for young gentlemen at Norton Lodge in Oystermouth, situated just a couple of miles from Swansea. Williams was a fervent disciple of 'muscular Christianity', and in March 1867, when he left the curacy of Port Eynon, his parishioners held a special reception for him, where a series of glowing tributes were paid. *The Cambrian* dutifully reported on this affectionate gathering, saying that Williams was 'a faithful minister of the gospel and a kind and sympathetic friend, ever ready to alleviate distress and promote the educational wants of the district.'

It was into Rev Williams' care that C.P. went in the autumn of 1868, and for the next few years, he was based in the genteel Swansea suburb of Mumbles, safely upwind of the town's industry and docks. There had been, at first, enough money in the family estate to keep him at Llandovery College, but with the family's coffers running low, Rev Williams decided that a more prudent course of action would be for him to be at Norton Lodge, where he could continue – at no cost – his studies in addition to further developing his skills as a cricketer.

If W.P.Whittington was the man who instilled a love of rugby in the impressionable youngster, it was William Bancroft and his son, also William, who helped to further cultivate C.P.'s abilities as a cricketer.[2] Born in Cambridgeshire in 1824, William senior had moved to London, and then on to Swansea to further his career as a boot-maker and a professional cricketer with the ambitious town club. He may have harboured dreams, when he was a young man, of securing a position at Lord's, but after moving to south Wales in the late 1850s, he quickly established himself as one of the leading professionals in the area, and was one of the earliest to introduce round-arm bowling to Welsh cricket fields. He played in several of the exhibition matches and other fixtures organised by the Glamorganshire club, formed in 1869.

---

2   William Bancroft (senior) was born in Barnwell, Cambridgeshire in 1821. He played cricket for Glamorganshire between 1861 and 1869, as well as appearing for several South Wales clubs including Swansea and Cadoxton. He died in Swansea in the summer of 1891. His son, William (junior), who was born in Bury St. Edmunds in March 1848, also appeared for Glamorganshire between 1864 and 1870, besides playing for the South Wales club between 1864 and 1886 as well as Radnorshire from 1869 until 1872. He also appeared for Swansea, Cadoxton and the Bryn-y-neuadd club in North Wales where he coached in 1883. William Bancroft (junior) also played for Glamorgan against Devon in 1891 at Swansea, and the following season appeared on the same ground in the trial match against a Colts side. He died in Swansea on April 26, 1906. Both of his sons also played cricket for Glamorgan – William James ('Billy') appeared regularly for the county between 1889 and 1914, with the all-rounder also appearing in first-class cricket for the West of England in 1910 and for South Wales in 1912. John ('Jack') kept wicket for the county in Minor County Championship games between 1908 and 1910, besides making nine first-class appearances in 1922.

William junior was also a talented cricketer, having benefited from the many hours his (no doubt) doting father paid to him at the Bryn-y-Mor ground which the town's cricketers used in the Uplands area, a mile or so away from Swansea Bay. Like other professional cricketers across the country, the Bancrofts helped to supplement their income from the town club with coaching the players at junior clubs in the area and also at the various academies and schools where cricket was encouraged.

C.P.Lewis could have had no finer tutors, as the Bancrofts coached the promising schoolboy and the other similar young gentlemen at the various academies in the area around Swansea, in the fashionable suburbs of Oystermouth and Mumbles. It was probably through the Bancrofts' suggestion that the burly youngster joined the Oystermouth club, allowing him to continue to play in a decent standard of cricket when the school term was over.

Tutorial influences.
Hugh Fowler's teaching and influence probably secured a place for Lewis at Jesus College, Oxford. Billy Bancroft senior (and later his son, also Billy) cultivated C.P.'s abilities as a cricketer, from the family base at St. Helen's, Swansea.

It also opened up other possibilities, as in the first week of August 1869, C.P. participated in the athletics meeting staged by the recently-formed Oystermouth club at their ground adjacent to the road leading to Langland Bay and described by the *Western Mail* as 'the snuggest of all the snug nooks with which this marine retreat abounds.' Many of the leading cricket clubs at that time held such events and the manly pursuits attracted a decent crowd, as many of the great and good of local society took the opportunity to see, and be seen, at the Sports Day.

The fifteen-year-old really enjoyed himself as he won two of the events – starting with the competition for throwing the cricket ball at a set of stumps fifty yards away. The teenager, plus two other club members each hit the wicket with one of their three throws in the first round, before hitting the stumps again in the throw-off which saw the youngster duly win the prize of a new cricket bat. Buoyed by his success in this first event, C.P. then participated in the second running event – a handicap race over 250 yards around the boundary of the cricket ground – and to his delight, and that of the watching Bancrofts, he beat his five rivals to win the race and add an impressive silver cup to his tally for the afternoon's sporting endeavour.

This rounded off an excellent summer for the fifteen-year-old. Back in May, he had been invited by Bancroft to play in a special match at Penmaen, where the cream of the talent from Norton Lodge joined with the scholars from Rev. John Colston's academy at Thistleboon House (where Bancroft also coached) to play a 'Gower XI'. It proved to be a successful match for young Lewis as the match report in *The Cambrian* described how 'the fielding of the boys was much admired and the bowling of C.Lewis and C.Buckley was highly effective.'

A few weeks later, he shone with the bat as the young gentlemen from the two Oystermouth schools defeated the Ffynone club. 'The highest scores were made by C.Lewis whose play was much admired,' reported *The Cambrian,* and he might have also played a hand in the defeat of the Swansea club by the Oystermouth club in August 1869. No scorecard survives, but perhaps it was Lewis who was instrumental in the Swansea cricketers being dismissed for 37 and 49 to give Oystermouth an innings victory.

Rev Charles Williams was also delighted by the progress that C.P. showed in academic affairs. Williams had attended Jesus College,

Oxford in the mid-1840s and he hoped that his talented nephew might one day follow in his footsteps. Indeed, there had been plenty of talk at Llwyn Celyn that C.P. might one day go up to Oxford, but given the financial situation of the Lewis family, he now required a scholarship in order for this to happen. Rev Williams was a gifted teacher, but other helping hands were needed if C.P. was going to secure a place at Oxford. Fortunately, Charles Williams had excellent contacts throughout south-west England, sending from Norton Lodge each year a number of pupils to leading public schools in England.

In particular, Williams had good links with Gloucester Cathedral School, which had a fine academic reputation and in February 1870 an agreement was made allowing C.P. to transfer to the Cathedral School at the age of sixteen and a half, allowing him to mix his final studies in theology and classics, plus cramming for the entrance exams at Oxford, with helping out with the coaching of sport at the school. It was not too much of a culture shock for the youngster, as there were other Welsh boys at the Cathedral School, which attracted boarders from leading families across south Wales who found it easy to travel to Gloucester by rail from Swansea, Cardiff and Newport.

Indeed, C.P. settled in very quickly into life at the Gloucester school, and in June 1870 – just four months after arriving – he was awarded the Fifth Form prize at the bi-annual prize-giving for, according to the Headmaster's citation in the *Gloucester Journal*, 'general proficiency in all subjects in the school.' He maintained this academic progress in subsequent months, adding the Sixth Form prize the following year as he proved himself amongst the top echelon of scholars at the school.

Founded in 1541 as one of King Henry VIII's less well-endowed cathedral schools, and now known as King's School, the Gloucester school had a deserved and growing reputation, thanks to the outstanding efforts of the head, Rev Hugh Fowler. A Cambridge classicist and mathematician, he had previously been headmaster of Bideford Grammar School before being appointed as the head of Gloucester Cathedral School in 1854. As one old boy, Frederic Hannam-Clark, later wrote in his memoirs, 'He was a first-rate Headmaster. Who will forget the wholesome fear he inspired in all the boys, big and little? Who will forget his heavy rapid stride through the schoolroom with his gown flying behind him, or his determinate twanging of the bell on his desk until he got silence?

The firm-set mouth, the searching eyes, the dignified bearing, the sonorous mouth – all had their effect upon the boys.'

Fowler was an outstanding teacher, and Lewis' success in the Oxford entrance exams owed much to the Headmaster's wise counsel. The two also shared a common interest in cricket, with Fowler being another disciple of the school of 'muscular Christianity' – so much so that fines that were levied on errant pupils went towards a fund for the levelling of the school's cricket field and the building of a small pavilion to house the cricket equipment as well as the boat which the school used on the adjoining River Severn.

At the time, the teaching staff at the school numbered just a handful, with Herbert 'Badger' Haines as Second Master, plus another gentleman who served as master in-charge of the choristers, and two other assistants. With 80 or so enthusiastic youngsters in their charge, it must have been a bonus to have the presence of the teenage sportsman, and perhaps his helping hand on the games field for rugby and cricket was part of the deal brokered with Rev. Williams, reducing even further his fees and helping his nephew build up his savings, which were likely to be heavily drawn upon at Oxford.

Despite the Headmaster's encouragement, the Gloucester school had quite modest sporting facilities in the 1870s, including a small gymnasium, known as 'Fowler's Shed', where wrestling, fencing and boxing took place, and a two-acre field where Kingsholm, the current home of Gloucester rugby club, now stands. It was, though, a far from ideal location, bounded then on one side by a noxious open sewer, whilst in the middle was a farm building called, not surprisingly, Castle Grim.[3] Some of the fields were levelled for a cricket square, though parts of the outfield remained uneven, but there was a general incline in a southerly direction towards the sewer, resulting in an unsavoury hazard for any boy sprinting after a ball, to say nothing of the subsequent task of fishing out the ball from the foul-smelling water. Despite these hazards, successful matches were played against two local clubs – Minchinhampton and Dymock – as well as Cheltenham Grammar School.

---

3   By way of contrast, the school's current playing field, Archdeacon Meadow, has staged a Gloucestershire first-class match each season since 1993, and other county matches since 1990.

Indeed against the latter in 1871 he almost single-handedly won the game for the Cathedral School after they batted first. Whilst other batsmen struggled on the Dean's Walk wicket, Lewis scored a magnificent 125 as the Gloucester school rattled up 218. Only two other batsmen got into double figures and, when the Grammar School batted, they were dismissed for just 14 and 26, with C.P. taking six wickets and a couple of catches. The Cathedral School won by an innings and 178 runs and as the *Gloucester Journal* rightly said, 'the victory was chiefly due to the superb batting of C.P.Lewis.'

Cathedral School, Gloucester in C.P.Lewis' time.

There were other ways as well by which C.P. might also have left his mark on cricket at the Cathedral School, especially through his big hitting in cricket practices. Indeed, the young Welshman might well have been the person responsible for the 'alleged damage to the roof of Mr Clutterbuck's house by cricket balls', as reported in the 1872 school accounts to the tune of £2 10s 8d.

A few games of rugby were also played against local schools, but without such a dynamic figure as W.P.Whittington, there were not as many matches as at Llandovery, with the emphasis at the

Gloucester school swaying more to academic and ecclesiastical matters. Indeed, exposure to the latter, with the daily services in the adjoining Cathedral, was probably another factor in Rev Williams' choice of 'finishing school' for C.P., for whom, like many younger sons, a career in the church might have been an option if he was unsuccessful in his Oxford exams. However, Williams need not have worried, and as a result of Fowler's outstanding teaching, C.P. subsequently won a place at Jesus College, Oxford, with formal and informal Welsh connections dating back to its foundation in 1571, as a Classics Exhibitioner[4] to undertake a four-year degree course, and it was here amongst the dreaming spires that he found his own religion in the expanding field of organised sport.

A truly classical education.
Lewis' entry - in Latin - in the Cathedral School register.

---

4   An exhibition was, and still is, a 'second-tier' scholarship, usually won through a competitive examination, where the recipient's tuition and other fees, and perhaps some living expenses, are paid for out of college funds. Exhibitioners are thus expected to show academic prowess.

Chapter Two
Oxford and a Lost Cause

C.P. went 'up' to Oxford University in October 1872 at the age of 19. It wasn't, however, until his fourth and final year in residence, in 1876, that he won a cricket Blue, as well as a half-Blue in athletics. Away from the lecture theatre and examination hall, his early years in residence seem to have been particularly devoted to sporting achievement for Jesus College, which at the time was one of the smaller colleges with just 60 undergraduates – significantly fewer than the 240 at Christ Church, 182 at Balliol, 156 at Exeter and 130 at Keble. Whilst it was easier for good sportsmen like C.P. to represent the smaller colleges, on the other hand the smaller colleges had less influence within Oxford's sporting hierarchy. This, and the fact that C.P. had attended relatively minor public schools, and hailed from a generally unfashionable cricketing locality, probably contributed to his failure to be selected for the freshmen's cricket trials in April 1873.[5]

As a result, he languished instead in inter-college sport until his final year in residence. His first appearance in the Jesus XI came on 23 April 1873, with C.P. batting at five in their line-up against Wadham College, and opening the bowling alongside Thomas Babington Jones, an outstanding schoolboy sportsman from Christ College, Brecon who, like his good friend C.P., was later a leading player in South Wales rugby. In 1873 Jones was on the fringe of the Oxford side, before winning a cricket Blue the following year, and for much of 1873 his medium-pace bowling alongside Lewis helped Jesus College secure a number of good victories in inter-college matches, as in the match against Wadham, when the latter were bundled out for just 34, with C.P. claiming four cheap wickets.

---

5   When C.P. finally received his Oxford Blue in 1876, by which time 440 had been awarded, he was only the fourth Welsh-born player to win one. His predecessors were his namesake W.H.Lewis, born in Pembrokeshire, who won a Blue in the first Varsity match in 1827; Morgan Jones, an Old Harrovian, born at Penylan, Cardiganshire who won Blues in 1849 and 1850; and C.P.'s close friend, Thomas Babington Jones, born at Maesteg, Glamorgan, who had received his Blue in 1874.

C.P. LEWIS
JESUS

Young hopeful.
C.P. as an undergraduate in 1875.

In 1874 C.P. moved up the college batting order to three – a position he retained for the remainder of his time in Oxford – but once again, it was his feisty bowling which caught the eye, with his best performance being eleven wickets in the two-innings match with Magdalen College, who were bundled out for 32 and 54 by the joyous Welsh students. The next year, he took nine wickets in an innings as Wadham were bowled out for a mere 19, followed by five- and six-wicket hauls against Exeter College and St Alban's Hall. He also struck an impressive fifty against the latter, but it was his bowling which earned C.P. an invitation to the final cricket trials on 10 May with Jones, no doubt, having sung his praises. C.P. duly appeared for the Next Sixteen against the Oxford XI, but despite taking five wickets he did not come any closer to selection for the Dark Blues in 1875, and remained in college games.

His reward finally came the following summer – one which saw Lewis in fine form for Jesus College with both bat and ball. By now he had settled for a pass degree – a general degree in arts – rather than take an honours degree in Classics, and had already taken papers in political economy and the 'Rudiments of Religion', a compulsory exam. His batting for the college in previous seasons had been full of promise, but he had yet to post any sizeable scores. In 1876 he blossomed into a hard-hitting No.3, scoring a memorable 206 against The Queen's College with his forthright strokeplay dominating the Jesus innings, and the match, with his double-century coming in a total of 331 and all on a wicket upon which only two other batsmen got into double figures.

With 102 against Oriel also under his belt, C.P. won selection for the final trials in 1876, and to his delight, was included in the Oxford side which opened its season at the end of May against M.C.C. on the Magdalen College ground at Cowley Marsh, as its

Lord's Ground.

R. B. Patterson, Lucas, Steel & Luddington are old Uppingham Boys !!

OXFORD V. CAMBRIDGE

MONDAY and TUESDAY, JUNE 26, 27, 1876.

OXFORD.

	First Innings.		Second Innings.	
A. J. WEBBE, Esq.....	c Shaw b Luddington	1	c Greenfield, b Patterson	16
F. M. BUCKLAND, Esq	c A Lytteltn.b Pattersn	32	c and b Luddington......	0
A. H. HEATH, Esq.....	b Luddington	0	b Luddington	0
T. S. DURY, Esq.........	c A.Lytteltn.bLuddingtn.	7	b Luddington	25
R. BRIGGS, Esq.	b Luddington	41	b Allsopp	32
A. PEARSON, Esq	b Patterson	0	b Luddington	14
W. H. GAME, Esq.	c Shaw, b Luddington	4	l b w, b Greenfield..... ...	109
D. CAMPBELL, Esq. ...	c Newton. b Patterson	6	b Greenfield	43
V. ROYLE, Esq.	c A.Lyttelton, bPatterson	2	not out	11
C. P. LEWIS, Esq.	c Greenfield,b Patterson	15	c Greenfield,b Patterson	1
H. G. TYLECOTE, Esq...	not out	0	b Greenfield	0
	b 2, l-b 2 w , n-b ,	4	B 5, l-b 3, w 2 n-b 1,	11
	Total............... ...	112	Total	262

CAMBRIDGE.

	First Innings.		Second Innings.	
F. J. GREENFIELD, Esq.	b Lewis.....................	1		
A. P. LUCAS, Esq.......	c Campbell, b Royle ...	67	*not out*	*23*
W. BLACKER, Esq. ...	b Lewis.....	0	*not out*	*0*
Hon. E. LYTTELTON	c Briggs, b Lewis	18		
D. Q. STEEL, Esq.......	c and b Royle	24		
Hon. A. LYTTELTON ...	c Briggs, b Pearson ...	43	*Each out*	*47*
W. S. PATTERSON, Esq.	not out......	105		
V. K. SHAW, Esq.	b Pearson...................	0		
H. T. ALLSOPP, Esq. ...	b Buckland	21		
S. C. NEWTON, Esq. ...	b Pearson	7		
H. T. LUDDINGTON,Esq.	b Lewis...................	6		
	B 4, l-b 5, w 1, n-b ,	10	B , l-b , w , n-b ,	*6*
	Total	302	Total	*76*

Umpires—Rylott and Farrands.   Scorers—Davey and West.

*** Special Telegraph Wires are provided for this Match, and messages can be despatched to any part of the United Kingdom from the Travelling Office stationed in the S.E. corner of the Ground.

A scorecard of the Varsity match of 1876, won by Cambridge by nine wickets. The annotation says that the Cambridge side included four Uppinghamians, a point picked up by H.S.Altham's History of Cricket, published in 1926. Lewis took four for 116 in the Cambridge first innings and none for 28 in the second.

Road for a quarter of an hour was one that will not readily fade from the memories of those who witnessed it. How the thousands from Lord's got on the "Underground" that evening this compiler knoweth not.' says the match report.

Batting for a second time, Oxford succumbed to 60 for five, but then a superb century by their captain W.H.Game, 'gallant if unavailing',[11] helped put them back in optimistic contention with an Oxford total of 262. At the start of the Cambridge second innings, Lewis found himself bowling to Lucas and the Hon Alfred Lyttelton with just 73 needed; they brought the total required down to 41 by the close of play. On the third day before a small crowd – it was still hot, but with a Cambridge win almost inevitable, only 576 came through the turnstiles – Lewis opened the bowling again, but no wicket fell until the scores were level, when Lyttelton ran himself out. Lucas then hit a boundary and so Cambridge won by nine wickets, their first win for four years. This is really the end of Lewis' first-class career, though he would have made no such distinction, as he was back at Lord's within a month to play against M.C.C. for the South Wales Club. The crowd was much, much smaller: now less a crowd, more a group of by-standers.

His selection in the South Wales line-up followed an appearance in the Club's annual trial match which in 1876 took place at the recently completed cricket ground at St. Helen's, and on the new lush turf which had been lain on the area of reclaimed sandbanks overlooking Swansea Bay. It was not much of a trial for C.P. who was dismissed lbw for 0, though there could have been no doubt that the Oxford Blue would make the touring side for the London tour if he was available.

Although he had spent so much time in Gloucester and Oxford, Lewis had also made a mark on the Welsh cricketing scene in the vacations perhaps to the detriment of his studies and seems to have thought of himself first and foremost as a Welsh cricketer. Llandovery Town Club had picked him to play against Knighton, the Welsh border town, where the leading player for the town and for the Radnor county side was Frank Cobden, whose fame rested on him winning the Cambridge *v* Oxford University match of 1870 by just two runs with a hat-trick. At Knighton on a Wednesday in

---

11   According to H.S.Altham in his standard *History of Cricket*, first published in 1926.

June 1874 – club matches often appear to be on market day at this period rather than weekends – Cobden scored 31 and 9, bowled each time by C.P.Lewis. Lewis had four wickets in the first innings, and eight in the second – nine of them bowled. Cobden, the nationally famous fast bowler, had just four wickets in the match.

Shortly after returning to Wales at the end of Trinity Term 1876, C.P. set off with the South Wales club on their London tour, which comprised of four two-day matches, three in London and one at Hove, spread over nine days in late July. He had 'qualified', though perhaps he had need to, by virtue of eleven wickets out of eighteen in the trial match at St. Helen's earlier in the month. The tour was a success for the club as well as for Lewis personally. The club won three matches, two by an innings, and one by five wickets. Lewis top-scored in three innings, including 120, his highest ever score for the club, in a total of 455 against the Surrey Club and Ground side at The Oval. In three of the matches his bowling was of little account, but at Hove he took five for 38 and then seven for 73 in a solid five-wicket victory for the touring side. His victims included six players who, in their time, played full county matches for Sussex.

Chapter Three
Undergraduate Athlete and Rugby Player

When Lewis was a young man, commercial, 'gate-money' sports, particularly those played in the winter months, existed on only a limited scale. The tiny numbers of mostly privileged undergraduates at the ancient English universities were disproportionately represented in any listing of the leading sportsmen of the 1870s, assisted by organisational preferences for 'amateurs'. University players packed the teams who played the first rugby internationals; Oxford University were finalists in the F.A.Cup competitions of 1873, 1874 and 1877; student athletes set new records in athletics events; and vast numbers of people identified themselves with Oxford or Cambridge at the time of the Boat Race. Even in cricket, which had a sizeable professional workforce, Cambridge University were plainly the strongest of any English first-class side in 1878. Though he himself had not attended one of the great English public schools where many of these leading sportsmen originated, C.P. had opportunities of sorts, while at Oxford, to achieve national sporting prominence. In cricket, as we have seen, he didn't quite achieve 'prominence', but in rugby he laid the foundations of an international career, and in athletics he represented the university, not very successfully, as we will see.

Little is known about how many organised games of rugby C.P. played whilst in residence at Oxford. As Jesus was a small college, it did not at this time have the manpower, or collective muscle, to raise its own team which could play larger colleges on reasonably equal terms. It is possible that C.P. may have participated in the combined college matches, or the scratch matches which were recorded without team lists in the *Oxford and Cambridge Undergraduates' Journal.*

What is known for sure, is that during his vacations from Oxford he played football and rugby in South Wales, both for Llandovery College and Llandeilo whilst back home with his eldest brother, as well as guesting for Swansea when he stayed with his uncle, Rev

Charles Williams at Norton Lodge. During the summer months, his visits to Oystermouth also allowed him to maintain contact with the Bancrofts, who no doubt further helped to hone his cricket technique with advice and encouragement about his batting and bowling.

He also became involved with Swansea Cricket Club. At the time the focus of their activities in Swansea was at Bryn-y-Mor Field – a large meadow, encircled by trees, opposite the Uplands Hotel. The proximity of the hotel was convenient – not just as a watering hole where the cricketers could celebrate a victory, or drown their sorrows, but also as a changing room and a place to hold meetings. Swansea had first used Bryn-y-Mor Field in 1868 after reaching an agreement with its owner Robert Eaton. Prior to this, the town's cricketers had led a peripatetic existence around the town using various fields, as well as wickets on Crumlin Burrows to the east of the town – an area which became home to a number of factory-run teams as the area became built up in the twentieth century – and also occasionally on a field at St. Helen's near Gorse Lane, overlooking Swansea Bay.

But the loss of these other locations in the mid-1860s posed major problems for the Swansea cricketers, so much so that they came close to disbanding because of the lack of a permanent home. Indeed, in August 1867, *The Cambrian* newspaper bemoaned that:

> the [Swansea] corporation – with such means at its disposal – does not make some provision for the healthful recreation of the inhabitants of the town. All available ground is being rapidly built upon. Why not therefore at once secure those (reclaimed) fields on the Mumbles road, by Gorse Lane, for a people's park – a part of which might be reserved as a cricketing ground?

Eaton's offer was a godsend, but the Bryn-y-Mor Field suffered from poor drainage, and there were many occasions in the late spring and early summer when the outfield was in a damp state. Nevertheless, the young gentlemen of the Swansea area so enjoyed their camaraderie on the cricket field that in 1872 they formed a football team – in fact, many cricket clubs in Wales at that time branched out into winter sports, playing either football or rugby.

On several occasions, Lewis joined with his friends from the Swansea Cricket Club in playing football on the cricket ground at Bryn-y-Mor. At first these games, which took place across both the square and the outfield, were tolerated by the cricketers, although as one later ruefully wrote 'football was played over the cricket pitch and consequently the wickets began to get in decent conditions about the end of August, if we were favoured with wet weather.' In 'fine weather they were never, at any time, fit to play on.'

There were occasions as well when the Bryn-y-Mor Field became so wet that the games were transferred onto the beaches a mile or so away in Swansea Bay. The young sportsmen also used Primrose Field, a ground in a more central location in the town which subsequently became the headquarters of Swansea's Working Men's Club. The Club for a while became an unofficial club house for the footballers, but the field they used had a pronounced slope, and there must have been several sighs of relief during the winter of 1874/75 when the new purpose-built and freely-draining facility at St. Helen's – as first suggested by *The Cambrian* correspondent in 1867 – became permanently available for both the ball games during the summer and the winter months.

Although they started out playing Association football during the winter months, they may also have played a few games of rugby. The hazards posed by the various pitches they used, and their damp nature, encouraged players to run with the ball in hand rather than kick it, as some of them had done on the rugby fields of their public schools and universities. These games of rugby steadily became more popular than football and in October 1874 – at the time of their move to St Helen's, and at the start of C.P.'s third year at Oxford – a motion was put to the members of Swansea Football Club that they should permanently adopt Rugby Union rules rather than those of Association football. The rugby code was then adopted, and a formal fixture list drawn up.

C.P. was one of the relatively affluent young gentlemen involved in these early games of rugby, and his contacts at Llandovery were no doubt behind the agreement to play home and away fixtures against the College from 1873. Interestingly, C.P. held qualifications to play for both sides, and who he played for in the autumn of 1873 is shrouded in mystery. However, for the 1874 encounter at Llandovery, he joined the College team as *The Cambrian* reported: 'Messrs Price, Williams, Jenkins, Lewis and little Davis contested the game pluckily and well for the College.' ... 'The Warden, Rev Watkins, acted as umpire and the match passed off without accident or dispute.' The *Western Mail* also records that 'Mr C.P.Lewis did the boys excellent service', confirming that the Lewis in *The Cambrian*'s report was indeed C.P.

Three weeks later, he was in the Swansea side which entertained Glamorgan Football Club at St. Helen's. The undergraduate was one of the forwards in the Swansea line-up which drew the game, despite according to *The Cambrian,* 'some very good runs and excellent scrimmaging. ... For Swansea, Meager, Richardson, Ingram, Lewis and Brown were perhaps the best. ... The play seemed to be highly appreciated by a large concourse of spectators, including many of the fairer sex.'

Although most of the participants in these rugby matches were well-to-do youngsters, there was, at times, nothing gentlemanly about the games which were quite dour and violent struggles, with few running moves and many mauls, where players wrestled with each other in trying to win possession of the ball, with their struggles, either rolling around on the floor or standing up, often carrying on for many minutes. Given this physicality, there was also some skulduggery, with contemporary reports, and letters written to the newspapers, complaining of the use of foul play, with attempts by some players to incapacitate prominent members of the opposing teams.

Whether C.P. revelled in this use of brute force is not known, but judging by the photographs that survive, he had plenty of upper-body strength and could probably look after himself if he was set upon or heavily tackled. He also was a quick runner, and it was these athletic skills, allied to his strength, that made C.P. a prominent figure as the game of rugby developed further in South Wales during the 1870s and 1880s.

His athletic skills also received recognition whilst he was up at Oxford, and whereas little is known about his rugby-playing when in residence, his record as an undergraduate in events for both Jesus College, and for the University team, reveal that C.P. possessed a range of talents in a variety of athletic pursuits. His debut in college athletics came in November 1872, as he participated in a number of races and events during the College's annual athletics day at the Marston Sports Ground. But it was the following year when his talents were rewarded as he finished second in the high jump, quarter-mile and mile races, besides winning the throwing the cricket ball event with a throw of 109 yards, 2 feet and 8 inches.

C.P. enjoyed even more success in November 1874 winning three events at the Jesus College Athletics Day – the shot-put, the long jump and the 110 yard hurdles – besides finishing second in the 100 yards sprint and the cricket-ball throwing event, as well as finishing third in the mile race. His growing confidence as a runner, and status within Oxford athletics, can also be gauged from the fact that during the term, he also appeared in various 'Stranger's Handicaps' held by other colleges on their own sports days, which were open to all of the University community. These races were ideal showcases for C.P. to display his prowess to a larger audience, and it must have given him much pleasure to finish second in races at Keble and St. John's.

In 1875 he won the Jesus College hammer and long jump events, throwing a distance of 85 feet, and jumping a distance of 18 feet 7 inches. He was also in the shot-put, high jump, and in quarter-mile and mile flat races. Indeed, his good form in these running events and in the 'Strangers' Handicaps', fuelled his ambitions of winning an athletics half-Blue. The sport was on the up at that time at Oxford, and in early March 1876 the University had to stage, for the first-ever time, a series of trials and qualification events so that the athletic elite from all of the colleges could qualify for the University's Athletics Sports later in the month.

The University Sports day was when selections for the match against Cambridge would be made, and C.P. duly took part in the high hurdles and hammer events, and secured qualification for these events on the opening day of the Athletics Sports, held on 25 March 1876 at the Marston Ground. It was a fairly successful day as he finished second in the hammer, throwing a distance of 94 feet 5 inches, and was runner-up as well in the 120 yards hurdles, beaten by one and a half yards by E.B.Nash of Lincoln College.

These performances earned Lewis a place as Oxford's second string in the hammer and hurdles events in the Varsity athletics match against Cambridge on 7 April 1876 at the Lillie Bridge track in West Brompton, London. In the words of *Jackson's Oxford Journal*, the event was 'in the presence of a very large and fashionable company', and perhaps this large gathering as well as the prestige of the event, slightly put C.P. off his stride, as in the hammer he failed to record a legal throw and finished fourth. He might have been pressing too hard to impress, but he might also have injured himself in attempting to throw as he did not run later in the afternoon in the hurdles.

However, it proved to be a good day for the rest of the Oxford athletes as they defeated Cambridge by six events to three. C.P. had played a very peripheral role in the Dark Blues' victory, but even so, it didn't stop him and his colleagues heading off into town to celebrate their team's success and the particular achievement of the Hon Marshall Brooks.[12] His celebrations also marked the end of his days as an Oxford athlete, and little did he know it at the time, his outstanding success in these sports at Oxford was also to play a major role in shaping the course of the next chapter in his life.

12   The meeting, attended by 12,000 spectators, (even though, not far away on the Thames, the free spectacle of the University Boat Race was also under way) is best known for the performance of the Oxford athlete, Marshall Brooks, who achieved 6ft 2½in in the high jump, jumping feet-first. *The Times* described this feat as 'unprecedented'. This is nowadays recognised as the then world record, although that concept was little developed at the time. Earlier in the year, at Oxford, he had cleared 6ft 0¼in, the first jump over six feet under 'regular' athletics-match conditions.

Chapter Four

Cricket for Breconshire and South Wales

By the time C.P. came down from Oxford his cricketing *curriculum vitae* – as an erstwhile Classicist, he would have appreciated the full Latin terminology – included a cricket Blue, plus appearances for the South Wales club and several Welsh county teams that had been formed during the 1860s and 1870s. These were boom years for cricket in South Wales, in which rural Carmarthenshire played a leading role. Indeed, the first recorded game of cricket in Wales had taken place in the county in August 1783 with a group of gentlemen meeting up at Court Henry Down near Cwmgwili, between Carmarthen and Llandeilo, for a challenge match.

Eighty years later, Carmarthenshire was at the forefront again, as a fully-fledged county club was created in 1864 by Charles Bishop who lived at Dolgarreg on the road between Llangadog and Llandovery. Within a few years, county teams representing Breconshire and Glamorganshire had also been formed, and like Bishop's side, they owed their origins to successful summer gatherings of well-to-do young gentlemen at various country estates where playing a few games of cricket was just one of the attractions and activities laid on by the hosts. Indeed, for some of the participants in these games, being able to bat or bowl was almost an irrelevance, given that many of the fair sex would be attending the banquets and balls which were held after the cricket was over.

Indeed, social reasons were also a factor behind the formation of the South Wales Cricket Club in 1859. After a few years of inactivity, the club was reformed in 1874 as a result of the emergence of some promising homegrown talent.[13] C.P. Lewis was

---

13 The South Wales club was best known outside the Principality in its earlier incarnation as the team which introduced W.G.Grace to higher-grade cricket in its 'London' tours of 1864 and 1865. In the first of these years, W.G., still only fifteen, famously scored 170 and 56* in a two-day match against the Gentlemen of Sussex on the Brunswick Ground on Hove seafront. In all, Grace played six matches for South Wales in July 1864, two of them at Lord's (his first appearances there), and three in July 1865, one at Lord's, by which time, now aged sixteen, he was a first-class player of some renown.

one of these 'bright young things', and during the mid-1870s, he enjoyed a rich diet of cricket, playing during term time for Jesus College and briefly for the University, before appearing during his vacations for Breconshire and the South Wales club.

On 24 June 1874, just after the end of his second year at Oxford, C.P. played his first match for Breconshire in their two-day game against Glamorganshire at Brecon. He batted at number three and ended up as top-scorer in the contest with 31 as Breconshire made 130, and dismissed the visitors for 43 and 44, with Lewis taking nine wickets in the game whilst his opening partner and friend from Jesus College, T.B.Jones, claimed eight as Glamorganshire lost by an innings. His friendship with Jones may well explain why C.P., with his roots in Carmarthenshire, was invited to play for Breconshire for whom he had no apparent qualification.[14] Llandovery, though, looks towards Brecon, fifteen miles to its east, rather than anywhere else in Wales, and it is perhaps an anomaly that they are in separate counties. In many respects they were twin towns – an analogy that is still relevant today – but it applies very readily in an era of poorer transport and mass communication.

The emergence of Jones and Lewis was one of the main reasons for the South Wales club being resuscitated in 1874, under the leadership of Glamorgan's founding father, J.T.D. Llewelyn. John Talbot Dillwyn Llewelyn was the son of a wealthy industrialist and former Mayor of Swansea, who lived to the north-west of the town at Penllergaer. Educated at Eton and Christ Church, Oxford, J.T.D. graduated in law and entered the Inner Temple in 1859. However, he opted against a legal career, and returned to south Wales where he went into business and politics, and in the course of the next fifty years or so, was a kindly benefactor to all kinds of sporting and social activity across the region.[15]

J.T.D. was a very useful cricketer himself, and as a lively round-arm bowler had once dismissed a young W.G.Grace whilst guesting in a

---

14   A year earlier, on 9 June 1873, seven English first-class counties, meeting at The Oval, had decided, among other things, that players were qualified to play only for counties where they were born or where they had lived for the previous two years. It is not clear, nor can it have been clear to Lewis and his fellow players, that they had intended the rules to apply to Welsh counties playing two-day friendly matches against one another.

15   He was later appointed High Sheriff of Glamorgan (in 1878) and followed his father as mayor of Swansea in 1891. After various unsuccessful attempts to enter Parliament, he was elected Conservative MP for Swansea, 1895-1900; he was created a baronet in 1890. He took great interest in secondary and higher education and was an active supporter of St. David's College, Lampeter, and of University College, Cardiff. He was a member of the Royal Commission which in 1896 examined the land question in Wales.

match against the West Gloucestershire club. He was also a capable batsman, but as far as cricket was concerned, perhaps his greatest asset was his vast range of contacts in the political, social and sporting world of Wales, as well as in the London area. Indeed, his wife, Caroline Hicks-Beach, was the daughter of a cabinet minister in various Tory governments, and the Llewelyns moved in very high circles.

Influence in high places.
J.T.D.Llewelyn, industrialist and politician, and, like C.P., a
pioneer of Welsh cricket.

Llewelyn was eager to see the emerging cricketers of south Wales earn wider recognition outside the region and, buoyed by the emergence of Lewis and Jones at Oxford, he arranged a series of fixtures in the London area, in 1874, so that the young Welsh gentlemen could go up to town and fly the flag for Welsh cricket. The London tour began with a two-day match at Lord's against M.C.C. Lewis' 28 was the top score in both innings, and he took six for 31 as M.C.C. were dismissed for 101 in the second innings, with all six wickets bowled. However, M.C.C. were still good enough to win the contest by 39 runs.

The tourists fared better in a one-day game against Prince's Club where the Welsh batsmen ran up 361 but, as declarations were not allowed then, it left their opponents little time to bat. In addition to their fine display of strokeplay, one of the highlights was the presence at the match of the then Prince of Wales, later King Edward VII. Two days later, against the Surrey Club and Ground at The Oval, Lewis took six for 51, including a return catch off H.H.Stephenson, the old Surrey professional who had led the first English tour to Australia in 1861/62. Arranged as a two-day match, it was all over in one: South Wales 119 and 45; Surrey Club and Ground 134 and 34 for 2.

Lewis' bowling record at this time reads rather like an old children's story in the *Victor* comic where Spofforth and his yorker appeared like Superman whenever there was a spot of bother. Lewis bowled many people, suggesting that his pace was too quick for many batsmen, even allowing for the rough pitches on which some of his games were played. However, his armoury also included a slower ball, as indicated by many cases of batsmen being dismissed caught-and-bowled. The many instances of lbw, and sometimes hit wicket, suggest that his pace and skill could certainly cut a swathe through mediocre batting.

After the London tour, Lewis' next recorded engagement was in a two-day match in mid-July for Breconshire against Glamorganshire at Cardiff Arms Park. Lewis opened both the batting and the bowling, and once again was top scorer in the match, making 58 in the first innings before being bowled by Arthur Redwood, a solicitor who was a leading member of Bridgend club. After taking two wickets in the Glamorganshire first innings, he bowled the top three in their second innings, including J.T.D.Llewelyn and two other prominent batsmen from leading clubs, before adding two more victims as the contest was drawn. Once again, a haul of seven wickets, plus his half-century, in a match against some of the best club cricketers in South Wales was a major feather in the cap of the 21-year-old undergraduate, and further evidence of his bowling prowess.

A week later he was playing for Breconshire against Herefordshire on the Hereford racecourse at Widemarsh Common. *Scores and Biographies* records he took six for 44 in the second innings as Herefordshire were bowled out for 34 and lost by 90 runs. Later in the season, he played in the return match at Brecon, scoring 25 out

T.B.Jones, a right-arm medium pace bowler, was a couple of years older than Lewis. Born at Maesteg, he attended Christ College, Brecon and Jesus College, Oxford. Like Lewis he won a cricket Blue: he played for and against Lewis for various cricket and rugby sides, particularly for Llandovery, until his death in Somerset in 1890, aged only 39.

of 85 and taking four for 21 in the second innings as Breconshire won again by eight wickets.

He was clearly in much demand as later in the summer he also played for Llandeilo Wanderers against Devynock and Sennybridge, the towns where the Tawe Valley meets the Tywi Valley. This was followed shortly afterwards by an appearance for the Gentlemen of South Wales against their professional equivalents, a two-day match at Neath, organised by the South Wales Club to emulate the Gentlemen *v* Players fixtures which were at the time amongst the most important in England. Lewis batted at number three and scored a majestic 112 out of 305, before taking six wickets in the Players' first innings. If evidence were needed of C.P.'s all-round abilities, it was clear to everyone at The Gnoll ground that the youngster could lay a strong claim to being the finest cricketer in south Wales.

In the following summer, 1875, between his third and fourth years at Oxford, C.P. went on the South Wales club's 'London' tour in early July, playing in three two-day matches, against M.C.C. at Lord's, the Gentlemen of Sussex at Hove and Surrey Club and Ground at The Oval. The visitors won only one of their matches, at The Oval, but here C.P. scored 64 facing the bowling of W.H.Game, who had already been elected Oxford captain for 1876.[16] It can have done his prospects for the next season little harm. On the

16   Game, a hard-hitting batsman and 'brilliant' outfield from Sherborne School, who was an exact contemporary of C.P., at Wadham College, had already won three cricket Blues and had some thirty first-class matches under his belt by this time. He had made appearances in August for the full Surrey side from 1871. He was also a rugby Blue and had a famously strong arm, having thrown the cricket ball 127 yards in the 1873 University sports.

tour overall, C.P. scored 136 runs usually batting well up the order, and took fourteen wickets at 19.07, opening the bowling in the first two games. Later in the season, he played twice for Breconshire against Glamorganshire, when, bowling with his Oxford colleague T.B.Jones, they dismissed their opponents for 47, 45, 84 and 102. Breconshire won both matches with some ease, C.P. taking fifteen wickets in all.

Chapter Five

Schoolmaster at Llandovery College

With his cricketing star most definitely increasing in magnitude, C.P. returned to Llandovery College in the autumn of 1876. Part of his job was to teach in the College's junior school, educating the young scholars aged from seven to thirteen in a variety of Classical topics. His main brief, however, was to oversee the teaching of athletic pursuits throughout the institution, especially amongst the older age groups. At the time there was just a handful of staff at the College, and it was quite a coup for the progressive school to secure the services of Wales' finest all-round sportsman. Typically he threw himself into his new duties with great enthusiasm, as one pupil later recalled, 'I have seen him transform, without a word, the lackadaisical efforts of a set of rabbits into irreproachable activity.'

To return to his old school, at a time when he had made so many contacts in the social and political world of south Wales, may have seemed a strange choice. With his academic[17] and sports credentials, he could have readily secured a teaching job at a prestigious public school in the English Home Counties or in the West Country, where he could have maintained links with the amateur side of first-class cricket and perhaps have become qualified for a first-class county.[18] Similarly he would have been in touch with English rugby clubs, then rapidly growing, but would of course have not been eligible for the English national side. During the University vacations, however, he seems to have been happy to spend his time in Wales or associating with specifically Welsh sporting endeavours. By teaching at Llandovery, he was able to

---

17 Though these were not of the highest, it has to be said. He passed two papers in the first term of his final year as we have indicated earlier. He passed classics papers in the Trinity (summer) Term of 1876, and finally history papers in the autumn term of 1876, by which time he had left Oxford, to satisfy the requirements for a pass degree. He had gone up to Oxford as an exhibitioner, expecting a good honours degree: no doubt his tutors shook their heads, regretting that he had spent too much time in sporting activities, both in term-time and during the vacations.

18 First-class cricket was not played in South Wales until 1910, and Glamorgan did not join the County Championship until 1921, both events rather later than an optimistic Welsh sports enthusiast might have expected in the 1870s.

stay fit and continue playing a decent standard of Welsh rugby and cricket. The offer to work at Llandovery stemmed from a friendship with the school's new Warden, the Rev Alfred George Edwards. The son of a clergyman from Merioneth, he had read Classics at Jesus College at the same time C.P. was in residence, and had played alongside him in the Jesus cricket eleven.

Under Edwards' energetic headship, Llandovery flourished with the number of pupils rising from just 27 in 1874 to over 180 by the 1880s. Edwards subsequently left the College to become the Vicar of Carmarthen: he was later a leading figure in the Church in Wales and eventually became the first Archbishop of Wales. By the time Edwards arrived at Llandovery, the influential W.P.Whittington had departed and there was a desperate need for an enthusiastic young master who could continue his good work, overseeing the sporting activities in the College and acting as a good role model.

Edwards had already persuaded another good friend from his days at Jesus, Charles Buckmaster – who had graduated in 1874 with a first in Natural Sciences – to teach at Llandovery, and having seen the way C.P. had shown similar excellence on the sports fields at Oxford, Edwards knew that Lewis would perfectly fit the bill to give sport at Llandovery a further boost. To Edwards' delight, his Oxford chum readily accepted the offer, with C.P. no doubt remembering how much he had enjoyed helping out with games at Gloucester Cathedral School.

There was plenty for C.P. to do, as the standard of rugby and cricket had dipped following Whittington's departure. Just a couple of months after C.P. started at Llandovery, the College suffered a heavy defeat in their rugby match against Swansea. The students conceded four tries and just to rub salt into the wounds, they could not put a full side into the field. However, this was the heaviest defeat for some time, as through C.P.'s guidance and coaching, he put his indelible mark on sport on at Llandovery, and with the number of students steadily rising, there were plenty of reserves to call upon.

He also made an impact in other areas of school life and it was a mark of his standing as both a schoolmaster and role model that within a couple of years he was invited to run Trafalgar House, a recently-purchased house to accommodate the overflow of boys seeking to board at the College. In previous years, the College coped with an overflow in numbers by renting lodgings in the town. But these boarders were largely unsupervised, and after lessons were over – and at weekends – the boys did as they pleased, some smoking and drinking heavily. Their actions brought many complaints, and with a surge in numbers, Edwards and the trustees of the College did not want a repetition. Their solution was to purchase a house in Stone Street, and invite C.P. to act as housemaster. He duly agreed and for the next few years looked after a dozen-and-a-half boarders, aged from fourteen to eighteen, with the help of a matron and another domestic servant.

His return to Llandovery also came at a pivotal time in the history of Welsh sport, with the 1870s being boom years for cricket and rugby in south Wales. During his time as a master at the College, C.P. played a major role at school, club and regional level, by coaching a host of promising scholars at Llandovery, playing for a variety of teams in west Wales and regularly appearing for the South Wales club, for whom he continued to serve as vice-captain and a most able lieutenant to J.T.D.Llewelyn.

The staff at Llandovery College in 1879.
Lewis, the young games master, is second from the left.

In his first summer back at Llandovery, he led the gentlemen of the South Wales club on their annual tour to London. It was quite an honour for the energetic young schoolmaster, at 23, to be given this role, but events on the field did not go entirely their way. At The Oval, they lost to the Surrey Club and Ground side by an innings with the county's professionals Edward Barratt, a left arm spinner from County Durham, taking eleven wickets, and fast left-armer Emmanuel Blamires obtaining nine more. In the previous match, against the Gentlemen of Sussex, C.P. took three in the first innings, and the only wicket to fall in the second as Sussex won by nine wickets after South Wales scored just 48 in their first innings. At Lord's, they fared little better in a twelve-a-side match as M.C.C. forced the Welsh to follow on, but they found a saviour in T.B.Jones, who scored 97 to help the visitors to the safety of a draw.

The 1877 season may not have been a great year for the South Wales C.C., but the following year they secured their biggest ever fixture. This was a plum match against the 1878 Australians whose tour was organised through their English agent James Lillywhite, jun. who had captained an all-professional side in Australia in 1876/77, playing in two representative matches later recognised as the first Tests. To secure a fixture with the Australians was a major coup for the South Wales club, and, in part, reflected the influence that both Llewelyn and Lewis held in the corridors of cricketing power. There is also further evidence of their influence in the choice of venue; the St. Helen's ground in Swansea, rather than at the Arms Park in the rapidly industrialising town of Cardiff and the ground used by the Glamorganshire side as well as the town club.

Llewelyn had helped to finance some of the costs incurred in the mid 1870s in creating the cricket field at St. Helen's, just a short drive by horse and carriage from his country estate at Penllergaer. He had been a kindly benefactor to other good causes in the Swansea area, and with Lewis of Llandovery as his right-hand man, it was fitting that this plum fixture should take place on the new wicket overlooking Swansea Bay.

Joseph Moore of Neath C.C., who served as secretary of the South Wales Club, reached an agreement with Lillywhite that the South Wales team would field eighteen players in a three-day fixture. But with the Australians playing an extensive series of fixtures spread throughout Great Britain,[19] this was subsequently amended to a

---

19   Between their first game which started on 20 May 1878 and their last which ended on 17 September, the Australians played forty matches in all. Twenty-one of these were against odds, mostly eighteens and twenty-twos, and nineteen were against other elevens, of which fifteen are recognised as first-class. The team comprised of twelve players, one of whom, W.E. Midwinter, made only ten appearances, after being 'repossessed' by Gloucestershire. The team thus played match after match with the side more or less unchanged.

two-day contest on Wednesday and Thursday, 10 and 11 July. This was squeezed in between a match which the Australians had agreed to play against the Orleans Club at Twickenham in West London on Monday and Tuesday, 8 and 9 July, and an odds match against an Oldham XVIII in Lancashire on Friday and Saturday, 12 and 13 July. Naturally, J.T.D.Llewelyn, as the figurehead of Welsh cricket and the man who had helped secure the fixture in the first place, agreed to lead the Welsh side, with Lewis as his trusty second-in-command. As a director of various railway companies, J.T.D. also persuaded a number of companies to run additional trains with reduced fares, allowing people from across the region to travel to St. Helen's to watch the tourists. His actions though may not have been entirely benevolent, because as a shrewd businessman, he realised the need for a decent crowd in order to meet the not inconsiderable sum of money guaranteed to Lillywhite in arranging the game, now reduced to just two days and without having the luxury of any gate money on a third day.

The task of sorting out the rest of the team largely fell to C.P.Lewis who, in keeping with the club's policy of representing each part of the region, sent invitations to a group of players drawn from across the area. To his delight, he received acceptances from the cream of the region's amateur talent, including Frank Cobden, the Cambridge Blue from the Radnorshire club. T.B.Jones agreed to turn out, as did two other mainstays of the Breconshire county side – Gerald Wontner, from the thriving Brecon Town and Garrison club, who had played provincial cricket in New Zealand, and Teddy Davies, a stalwart of the Brecon and Crickhowell clubs who was one of the finest wicket-keeper batsmen in South Wales at that time. The Swansea club were represented by Charles Chambers, a forthright batsman who later became President of the town's Rugby Club and the first President of the Welsh Rugby Union, together with Lewis Jenkins, a solid batsman who eleven years later had the honour of opening the batting for Glamorgan C.C.C. in their inaugural county match.

The Carmarthenshire area was represented by G.B. ('Jerry') Elkington, a forcing top-order batsman from Burry Port and an electric fielder, whilst Monmouthshire's representative was Henry Ivins, a left handed hitter and slow bowler. Another who agreed to appear was Edward Ord, a dependable batsman who played for the Cadoxton club from Neath, along with teenager Robert Knight, an outstanding schoolboy batsman from Clifton College, Bristol and

Bridgend C.C. who had just won a place at Oxford, where he subsequently won three Blues in cricket and rugby.

The Cardiff club had several representatives – Edmund David, a fine all-rounder for St Fagans C.C. and a man who in 1889 would lead Glamorgan in their first fixture; Francis Dickenson, another forcing all-rounder; Edwin Jones, a middle order batsman and one of Cardiff's leading stockbrokers; Cuthbert Riches, a steady opening batsman, who was an engineer with the Taff Vale Railway; Bertie Young, another cricketing engineer, who was a prolific opening batsman; and Alex Morris, a free-scoring batsman with a fine record for the Cardiff club. The South Wales line-up was completed by acceptances from Edward Bannerman, a Scottish batsman who had played for Shropshire and was working in south Wales, and from E.W.Curteis – who had played first-class cricket for Kent and had helped organise the South Wales club's annual tour to the south-east – who was in Wales on military duty. A fair side, C.P. must have thought, with five players who had played first-class cricket, and the cream of Principality club cricket.

While C.P. was organising his side, the Australians were criss-crossing the country on their tour. By the time they reached Swansea in mid-July they had already played fourteen games in seven weeks, appearing in Nottingham, then London, back up to Yorkshire, then Birmingham, back to London, up to Leeds and Sheffield, across to Stockport, back to London. On and on they went, a dozen young men – seven of them under 25 – creating the enduring legend of competitive Australian cricket, with its fast bowling, fine outfielding and, inevitably, umpire-goading. Most famously, they had beaten M.C.C. in a single day, dismissing the premier club for 33 and 19,[20] with Spofforth and Boyle taking nineteen wickets between them. Spofforth, 'the demon bowler', bowled with a very high action, rarely seen before in England, and undisguised hostility, leading elderly journalists to refer to 'frenzy' and 'maddened crowds'.

The week leading up to their prestigious fixture in Swansea saw Lewis organize several practice sessions as the young Welshmen prepared for the challenge of taking on the tourists, whose exploits across England had attracted much press attention. But, as the days ticked by, rumours started that the Australians, whose

---

20   A match aggregate of 52, at the time the second lowest ever recorded by one
      team in a completed first-class match.

The famous Australian touring side of 1878, which beat the M.C.C. in a single day's play, on 27 May of that year.
Standing (l to r): J.M.Blackham (wk), T.P.Horan, G.H.Bailey,
J.Conway (manager), A.C.Bannerman, C.Bannerman, W.L.Murdoch.
Seated: D.W.Gregory (captain).
On the ground: F.R.Spofforth, F.E.Allan, W.E.Midwinter, T.W.Garrett, H.F.Boyle.

fame and success were each increasing, would not bother to come to Wales, preferring instead more lucrative matches elsewhere in the United Kingdom. The day before the game one newspaper even reported: 'It is now stated that the Australians will not be able to come to Wales, as they are engaged in London.' Perhaps there were concerns over the guarantee that J.T.D. had promised, but as it turned out, nobody should have worried as Gregory and his men honoured their commitment and travelled by train from Twickenham through the night to reach Swansea. They had cut short their match with the Orleans Club after only two days' play. It was hardly the best of preparations, and no doubt influenced J.T.D. when he won the toss and, after discussing things with Lewis, decided to bowl first against the tourists. Here faithfully reprinted is how the events unfolded as reported by *The Cambrian*, considered at the time to be the national newspaper of Wales:

CRICKET MATCH
THE AUSTRALIAN CRICKETERS AT SWANSEA
THE COLONIAL XI v XVIII OF SOUTH WALES

The Australian cricketers have created an almost unprecedented stir among the leading exponents of the National Game of England, as they have borne off the laurels from so many well-contested fields, that their advent to South Wales was looked forward to with a very great deal of the most lively interest which was not confined to the notaries of the game, but extending itself to the general population.

The Marylebone Club, ruling the roost at the headquarters of cricket in England (Lord's Ground, London) no doubt has as high an opinion of their own prowess as the country generally; and when they and other of the principal home clubs had been beaten on their own grounds by the Colonial team, the newspapers teemed with criticisms on their play, and the public mind was seized with a natural curiosity to see these men whom Australia had sent forth to put the old country through its facings in the exposition of excellent cricket.

For some years past Swansea and South Wales generally have been awakened to the life of cricket, and praiseworthy efforts have been made by public men, notably by Mr J.T.D. Llewelyn, the High Sheriff of the County, to train up a lot of cricketers who shall uphold he honour of the Principality in the friendly rivalry of bat and ball. The men of South Wales have felt themselves sufficiently strong to challenge competition with severable notable teams, and they wisely determined to measure their prowess against that of the Australians.

The match came off on Wednesday and yesterday on St. Helen's ground. It was at one time thought that we should be disappointed – that the Colonists could not reach us after the game at Twickenham in time to keep their appointment, but by dint of travelling all night they arrived at Swansea at 4.30am on Wednesday morning, and came to the field as fresh as if they had enjoyed a full night's rest.

The only change in the constitution of the team was that Mr Conway[21] played instead of Mr Allan – presumably to give that gentleman a rest before they play forthcoming important events. The team have worked hard since they have been in England, frequently travelling all night and playing all day.

There was a very numerous attendance on Thursday, it being estimated that no less than three thousand persons witnessed the play from the raised promenade, from private carriages, and from the other parts of the field. The weather was enjoyably fine throughout the day.

Wickets were pitched at 11.30 according to the announcement. Mr J.T.D. Llewelyn won the toss, and after some consultation with his men, it was decided to send the Australians first to the wickets. The arrangement was favourable to the visitors because by it they had the best of the day's light. Play commenced about 11.40 when the brothers Bannerman went first to the wickets for the Australians, to the bowling of J.T.D.Llewelyn and C.P.Lewis. C.Bannerman made an admirable cut for four from the first ball of the captain's first over, and A.Bannerman treated that bowler in the same way in his second over.

Defective fielding at short leg then gave C.Bannerman a three off C.P.Lewis' bowling. Here the South Wales wicket-keeper E.G.Davies was disabled by a ball which cut the flesh between his thumb and forefinger, and his place was filled by E.David of Cardiff. T.B.Jones replaced Llewelyn as a bowler, and his first over was a maiden. C.Bannerman, however, played his balls to advantage, and soon hit him to the boundary, drove him for two, and cut him for four, these achievements being deservedly applauded.

Having been badly missed at short slip C.Bannerman made another couple and then was clean bowled by C.P.Lewis for a good 27, played in excellent form. One wicket for 37. Horan took C.Bannerman's place, and the scoring slackened. The bowlers were changed, F.C.Cobden taking Lewis' place and Lewis Jenkins the other, when the telegraph showed 58.

---

21   John Conway, the Australians' manager, aged 36, who played in four other matches on the British part of the tour, and three further matches when they travelled on to America. He had previously played nine first-class matches, mostly for Victoria, and later appeared for Otago.

A.Bannerman was caught by his South Wales namesake at third man after having played carefully for 17. Two wickets for 60.

The Australian captain, Gregory, was caught at short leg before he had scored any. Three for 60. Garrett succeeded him, and as he and Horan drove the slows to the boundary, J.T.D.Llewelyn resumed bowling at the same end as before. This bowler's third over being hit for 8 runs, however, brought T.B. Jones as a substitute. Garrett made a fine cut to the boundary off Cobden, and a nice bit of fielding by Riches eliciting applause.

A subsequent over of Cobden's resulted in a cut for 2, a drive for one, and a leg hit for 4, and when the 100 was here put up the Australians were loudly cheered. C.P.Lewis replaced T.B.Jones as a bowler, and was cleverly hit to leg for 4 by Horan. Cobden bowled Horan off his thigh, and he retired amid applause, having made five 4s and five 2s, and contributed 38 to the score of 119. Four wickets for 119 when the lunch bell rang.

Play was resumed with Garrett and Murdoch batting. With the second ball of the first over Cobden put Garrett out, who had made a good 25 and showed some hard hitting. Spofforth, the great bowler, then walked to the wickets. He ran some byes, snicked for 4; put up one between the wickets which the fielders failed to secure, and then was bowled by Cobden with a shooter. Six wickets for 138, of which the last made 8.

After some quite steady play Bailey made a forward cut for 3, and Murdoch a cut to the boundary, when the latter's leg stump was taken. Conway then took the bat, and some singles were made from the frequently changing bowlers. Bailey played splendid cricket, with some good cuts and drives. Conway was easily caught off Lewis. Eight for 194.

At four o'clock the 200 was put up and cheered. Blackham came in next. Bailey drove Jenkins to the deep long on for 4, and then Blackham was easily caught in the slips. Boyle, the last man, made a fine draw off Lewis for 5, and then Bailey was bowled by a shooter. The innings concluded at 4.15 pm for 219, to which Bailey had contributed 45. The wicket was fast, and the batting of the visitors was rather steady and effective than brilliant. The fielding of the South Wales team was somewhat loose, with the exception of that of Elkington, Riches and Bannerman; and the laurels of the bowling belong to Cobden and Lewis.

Cuthbert Riches and H.Young went first to the wickets for the Eighteen to the bowling of Spofforth and Boyle, who remained at their posts throughout the innings. Young scored 2 by a draw, and then Riches played one into the hands of point. One wicket for 2. Elkington succeeded and made a pretty cut for 2 off Spofforth. The result of the first ball of Boyle's next over was that Young was finally caught by Gregory (captain) low down at slip. Bannerman next came in. Elkington was caught at the wicket and replaced by Cobden, whose middle stump was clean bowled by Spofforth's first ball. Four wickets for 6 runs.

Capt Curteis then came in. Bannerman was caught at long on from a leg hit, and T.B.Jones, coming to the wicket, drove Boyle along the ground for 3, and was then bowled in revenge. C.P.Lewis, the next man, made a high hit which was barely missed, as was also a high drive by the same man off Spofforth. This bowler put in a very fast ball, which sent Lewis' stumps springing out of the ground. Seven for 40. L.Jenkins then went in. Capt Curteis was bowled by one of Boyle's curly deliveries. Eight for 42. Wontner succeeded. Jenkins was snatched at point. Nine for 45. Wontner was caught behind the bowler. Ten for 46. Morris made a good on drive for 3 and Chambers hit Boyle to the boundary. Spofforth's next ball took Morris – 11 for 57 – and J.T.D.Llewelyn (the captain) then came in amid the cheers of the field, but soon patted a ball into the hands of point. E.David made a good hit to square leg for 4; was then missed at mid off; but was easily caught and bowled by Spofforth in the next over. Thirteen for 75.

Dickenson succeeded him, and later on was magnificently caught by Horan after he had scored 10. Chambers played very steadily, and maintained his place longer than any one of his team but was, at length, bowled by Spofforth after making 8. Ord was vanquished by Spofforth's first ball, and the innings closed at about half past six, when the telegraph recorded 94. The fielding of the Australians was very good and the disposition which the Captain made of his men was unusual and most effective. Spofforth, the great bowler, has a most peculiar and impressive action, throwing his arms about like the sails of a windmill, and deceiving the batsmen by delivering many a moderate ball with all the appearance of a very fast one.

After play was over, a banquet was held in Swansea at which the Australians were guests of honour with a series of toasts being made to the various individuals who had organised the fixture. After his efforts in helping to raise the South Wales team, a toast was drunk to C.P.Lewis, but the banquet proved to be quite a rowdy and noisy affair, and the newspaper reported that Lewis responded 'briefly and inaudibly'.

No doubt most heads had cleared by the time that play resumed the following morning at 11.30 am, but it was definitely a case of after the Lord Mayor's show, as the South Wales XVIII were bowled out four hours later for just 88, giving the tourists a comprehensive innings victory. The correspondent from *The Cambrian* newspaper, who had eulogised about the talents of the home side in the lead-up to the game and in his first innings report, was much more sparing with his comments, writing that 'There was nothing of particular note in the playing of The Eighteen today. The best play was shown by Messrs Riches, Chambers, and L.Jenkins. ... The bowling of Spofforth and Boyle was very good today, the latter carrying off the palm.' The final scorecard read:

Australians

A.C.Bannerman	c E.Bannerman b Cobden	17
C.Bannerman	b Lewis	27
T.P.Horan	b Cobden	38
*D.W.Gregory	c Llewelyn b Cobden	0
T.W.Garrett	b Cobden	25
W.L.Murdoch	b Lewis	10
F.R.Spofforth	b Cobden	8
G.H.Bailey	b Lewis	45
J.Conway	c and b Lewis	12
†J.M.Blackham	c E.Bannerman b Lewis	5
H.F.Boyle	not out	5
Extras		27
Total		219

Bowling: Lewis 30.3-5-60-5; Llewelyn 21-10-33-0; T.B.Jones 19-7-36-0; Cobden 28-13-41-5; Jenkins 8-2-22-0.

South Wales Club

H.H.Young	c Gregory b Boyle	2	c Blackham b Spofforth	0
C.H.Riches	c Bannerman b Spofforth	0	not out	5
G.B.Elkington	c Blackham b Spofforth	2	c Bailey b Boyle	0
E.M.Bannerman	c Murdoch b Spofforth	6	b Spofforth	13
F.C.Cobden	b Spofforth	0	b Spofforth	5
E.W.Curteis	b Boyle	12	c Blackham b Spofforth	2
T.B.Jones	b Boyle	5	c Murdoch b Boyle	6
C.P.Lewis	b Spofforth	11	c Boyle b Spofforth	2
L.Jenkins	c C.Bannerman b Boyle	3	c Boyle b Spofforth	15

G.Wontner	c Garrett b Boyle	3	b Spofforth	3
C.C.Chambers	b Spofforth	8	lbw b Boyle	2
A.W.Morris	b Spofforth	5	b Boyle	8
*J.T.D.Llewelyn	c C.Bannerman b Spofforth	0	st Blackham b Boyle	9
E.U.David	c and b Spofforth	8	c Garrett b Boyle	1
F.D.Dickenson	c Horan b Boyle	10	c Bannerman b Boyle	0
E.W.Jones	not out	2	b Boyle	2
E.Ord	b Spofforth	0	b Boyle	0
†E.G.Davies	absent hurt		absent hurt	
Extras		17		15
Total		94		88

Bowling: First innings: Spofforth 26.1-11-35-10; Boyle 26-9-42-6.
Second innings: Spofforth 31-13-40-7; Boyle 31-19-33-9.

*Edmund David, who acted as the South Wales Club's
emergency wicket-keeper against the Australians in
1878, and eleven years later led Glamorgan in their
inaugural match at Cardiff Arms Park.*

Chapter Six

A Cup Held Aloft

After their game with the Australians, the remaining matches held by the South Wales Club in 1878 were inevitably something of an anti-climax. On 3 June they had held their annual trial at Swansea prior to the London tour. Lewis scored 20, and took six wickets in the first innings, followed by three in the second. The game, though, featured few of the region's leading players, as many were unable to get time off to play either in the trial at St. Helen's or the games on the London tour. With several new faces in the South Wales side, including Edward Hill, a colonel in the Glamorgan Militia and a prominent figure in local politics, C.P. did not play at Lord's and gave others a chance to play on the hallowed turf. He returned to the side for the match at Hove, taking four wickets in one innings and five in the next. The two-day game against the Gentlemen of Sussex drew a sparse crowd, and there were few people on the ground to see the South Wales side dismiss the home side for 79 *en route* to a handsome victory by 142 runs.

Lewis continued to play with great success for the Llandovery Town side and, as was the custom at that time, the College side as well. Against Christ College, Brecon he made 18 out of 36, a total which was less than half the opponents 79. Against Cowbridge Grammar School he scored 26 out of 103. Cowbridge got 126 thanks to a batsman called Crosby who went for the bowling. 'He gave three hard chances, but such hitting,' said one newspaper.

In 1878 the College also played Sennybridge, down the valley towards Brecon, but never noted for cricketers. They were bowled out for 13 and 11, with Lewis running amok through their batting line-up. It was a similar story when he played for the College against the Town, who made just 10 and 35. There were eight ducks in the Town's total of 10, and, though no bowling figures or dismissals are recorded, we can guess who was the bowler chiefly responsible. In July, Builth Wells came to Llandovery and Lewis made 129 out of their total of 332. Poor Builth got just 32, once again failing to come to terms with Lewis' bowling.

Despite the heavy defeat by the Australians, J.T.D. and the other committee members of the South Wales C.C. were quite heartened by the state of club cricket. But it was clear that further improvements could be made, and the committee decided to promote an inter-club competition. Lewis believed that a more competitive approach between clubs was needed and after a lengthy, and at times quite excited, discussion about the success of a similar idea already put in force by the region's rugby players, the South Wales C.C. in 1879 instigated a Challenge Cup for the region's cricket clubs.

A well-known firm of silversmiths, Elkington and Co of Birmingham, were invited by C.P. to make the cup – a choice possibly based on the fact that one of the leading Welsh players, Jerry Elkington of Burry Port copper works, was related to the owners of the Birmingham company. Both the College and Llandovery Town entered for the first year, but the Town could not raise a side and pulled out of the first-round tie with Cadoxton. Some fixtures were played at neutral venues, with Llanelli and Brecon meeting at Llandovery, whilst Llandovery College played Newport at Swansea. The men of Gwent were humiliated by C.P. and his scholars, who bowled them out for just six runs. Lewis had six wickets – all bowled. Earlier Lewis had made 42 not out of 55. Second time round, he failed as the school made just 24. Owen Jones, who was his best cricketing pupil and would go on to be a Glamorgan stalwart in the 1890s, top-scored with 5. Newport then got their heads down and won the match by seven wickets, with the future Welsh rugby international George Harding making an unbeaten 31.

Lewis continued his decent form on the 1879 London tour, as the Gentlemen of Sussex were beaten by the South Wales club by eight wickets. Lewis claimed four scalps, but his team then lost to Surrey Club and Ground, a side with eight first-class players aboard. 'The visitors were in every way overmatched. Mr Shuter played a slashing innings and hit 50 out of 70. His hitting was brilliant in the extreme,' said *The Cambrian* newspaper of the Surrey player's second innings. Lewis made 10 and 39, and took just one wicket, but he fared better against M.C.C. at Lord's, taking seven wickets in the match. It didn't, though, lead to a Welsh victory as a century from Lord Anson laid the foundations for a 256-run win for M.C.C. That the M.C.C side included eight players who had appeared in first-class cricket, or would later do so, including Wilfred Flowers and William Mycroft, two 'heavyweight' professionals of the era, is a measure of the premier club's assessment of their Welsh opposition.

The South Wales fixture list for 1879 also included home and away matches against the Clifton Club – the leading side in the Bristol area. Lewis missed the match in Bristol, but turned out for the second, staged at Rodney Parade in Newport alongside the rugby ground on the steep, muddy banks of the River Usk. Clifton included six first-class cricketers in their side. Lewis scored 24 at number five, but the match was ended by the weather on the first day with the South Wales team on 186 for five.

Llandovery College enjoyed a good run in the Challenge Cup in 1880, and all after having a lucky escape in the first match, once again against Newport at the neutral venue of Swansea. Newport scored 145, with 53 from Harding. When Lewis was dismissed for just three it looked all over, but two tail-enders added 70 and held on for a draw at 117 for nine. It was enough to get Llandovery a replay, and next time around they turned the tables: Llandovery 233, Newport 55.

Their next opponents were the powerful Cadoxton club which J.T.D.Llewelyn – whose first home was in the area – had resurrected in March 1863 from the wreckage of the now defunct Neath club whose finances had taken too many big hits after an overambitious committee had arranged a series of exhibition matches the previous decade against the All England Eleven. After several years of inactivity, J.T.D. breathed new life into the organisation, paying the rent for the use of the lavish grounds of Gnoll House, the home of the owner of the town's copperworks, and hiring, entirely at his own expense, a professional. With one of the grandees of Welsh sport as their patron, the Cadoxton club rapidly expanded its operations. Within a couple of years, they had over 120 members, including most of the major figures in the social and political world of south Wales, plus a fixture card which listed games against other leading clubs such as Swansea, Llanelli, Brecon and Cardiff, as well as by the end of the decade a match against M.C.C. at Lord's.

To play the premier club in the region, and a side regarded by many as 'the M.C.C of Wales' was perhaps quite a daunting prospect for the Llandovery students, especially as they had won the Challenge Cup the year before. But they had been well prepared by C.P., and their talismanic tutor was in fine form himself, top-scoring in the match with 56 – Owen Jones made 35 – out of 126, before being the leading wicket-taker as Cadoxton replied with just 37 and 24. Llandovery thus won the contest comprehensively, held again at St. Helen's. Lewis had six wickets in the first innings, though other bowlers were used in the second.

A bye – an odd position in the progress of the tournament to have such an arrangement – then put Llandovery straight into the final at the Arms Park on 30 and 31 July, against a Cardiff side chock-full of the leading players in the region, and colleagues of C.P. in the South Wales eleven. Besides Edmund David, the Riches brothers and Edwin Jones, their side also included J.P.Jones – a leading architect in the Taff-side town and, like C.P., an enthusiastic supporter of rugby. In the course of the next few years, Jones also became a pivotal figure in the creation of Glamorgan C.C.C., drawing wisely on his many friends in the social and political world, as well as his colleagues from the South Wales club.

C.P. contributed little if anything to the formation of the Glamorgan county club. There are now no records as to why Lewis and Jones did not see eye to eye when a fully fledged county side was formed, so there may be much more – hidden, perhaps for ever, in the mists of time. The entries in the scoresheet, reproduced below, show how Lewis dismissed Jones in each innings, and then by virtue of his first innings score of 40, became top-scorer in the match. Indeed, Jones was one of nine victims for Lewis, and through his efforts with bat and ball, the scholars were left needing just 33 to win the Cup. But Edwin Jones then produced one of the most devastating spells of bowling ever seen at the Arms Park, as he took nine for 10 with the youngsters being bustled out for just 14. C.P. departed for a duck, and we can only wonder whether a few caustic words were exchanged between the proud schoolmaster and the Cardiff architect, when Lewis returned to the pavilion with his dream of winning the Challenge Cup with his young charges now lying in tatters as Cardiff won the cup by 18 runs.

Cardiff

W.H.Williams	b C.P.Lewis	7	b O.Jones	3
E.U.David	b C.P.Lewis	5	c Evans b C.P.Lewis	0
W.L.Yorath	not out	1	b Jones	4
A.E.David	b C.P.Lewis	7	b O.Jones	12
J.P.Jones	b C.P.Lewis	2	b C.P.Lewis	19

H.F.Calcutt	b O.Jones	17	b O.Jones	0
Cuthbert Riches	run out	2	not out	3
Chas. Riches	c C.P.Lewis b O.Jones	2	b O.Jones	0
E.W.Jones	b O.Jones	2	b C.P.Lewis	2
B.Jones	b C.P.Lewis	3	b C.P.Lewis	5
C.N.Berkeley	lbw b O.Jones	0	b O.Jones	3
Extras		13		9
Total		61		60

Bowling: First innings: C.P.Lewis 29.1-19-20-5; O.Jones 23-13-13-4; H.E.Lewis 7-1-15-0.
Second innings: not known.

Llandovery College

J.Carver	b Chas Riches	12	c Chas Riches b E.W.Jones	4
A.L.Rowlands	not out	12	c David b E.W.Jones	0
C.P.Lewis	c E.W.Jones b Chas Riches	40	b E.W.Jones	0
G.T.Evans	b E.W.Jones	0	b E.W.Jones	0
A.E.Kempthorne	c sub b B.Jones	17	b E.W.Jones	0
O.Jones	c Cuth Riches b B.Jones	9	b E.W.Jones	3
F.C.Cornish	b Williams	0	run out	3
D.S.Jones	b Williams	1	lbw b E.W.Jones	0
E.J.McLellan	lbw b Williams	0	not out	2
J.O.Evans	b B.Jones	1	lbw b E.W.Jones	0
Extras		7		0
Total		89		14

Bowling: First innings: Williams 40.1-5-14-4; B.Jones 30-3-33-3; Berkeley 4-0-13-0;
E.W.Jones 40-9-6-1; Chas Riches 8-3-16-2.
Second innings: Williams 21-18-4-0; E.W.Jones 22-15-10-9.

Members of the Cardiff club were clearly becoming more influential amongst the hierarchy of the South Wales C.C. as the Arms Park became the venue for three important matches. The South Wales club's 1880 season started off with the usual annual trial, a probable eleven versus a possible eighteen, for the 'London' tour. Although rain washed out the second day of the match at Cardiff, Lewis took seven of the eighteen's wickets, with three bowled and one hit wicket. Clifton were the first high-profile visitors to play the club at the Arms Park. It was relatively easy for their players to travel by train to Cardiff, and despite improvements to the train timetable, it was still quite a trek for them to play at St. Helen's or further west, much as Lewis and Llewelyn would have dearly liked. Nevertheless, it proved to be a good match for Lewis against the Bristol side as he took five for 34 in the first innings, and then three more in the second, before making 39 as he led his side to a five-wicket victory.

A couple of weeks later M.C.C. played at the Arms Park. This was their first out-match against South Wales, played at the now rapidly developing Cardiff ground, where facilities had improved through the encouragement of the third Marquess of Bute – the aristocratic tenant of Cardiff Castle and the owner of several of the docks which had brought great fortune both to him and the town. A wooden pavilion plus a decent wicket and practice nets, tended by the Cardiff professional, had been created, and this brought great benefit to the Cardiff players and other teams who, like the South Wales club, were granted permission to use the ground by the Marquess. But M.C.C., flying the flag with a side which included nine first-class cricketers, proved to be far too strong for the South Wales gentlemen. Lewis scored 27 and 23 – he was run out yet again in the second innings – and, opening the bowling, took two for 64 as M.C.C. won by an innings.

The 'London' tour followed at the end of August, rather later than usual, with the return match with Clifton taking place on Durdham Down, Bristol, on their way home. At Hove, the Gentlemen of Sussex won a close match by 13 runs. Lewis took three wickets in the first innings and four in the second, but the Welsh side fell short when left 131 to win. The Lord's match was drawn. Lewis did little with the bat, but claimed eight wickets in the first innings and five out of only eight which fell in the second. His bowling form continued against Clifton, where he took eight for 62, plus two more wickets in the second innings. After being bowled out for 94 in their first innings and conceding a lead of 20, South Wales lost by 61 runs. Now 27, it is probable that C.P. was at about the peak of his powers as a bowler. In the three matches on this tour, he took 30 of the 58 wickets to fall to his side, and sixteen of them were players who had appeared in first-class cricket. He had played regularly earlier in the season for the college and for the Llandovery Town side when the school closed for the summer. No doubt he bowled regularly in the nets to the College boys, honing his skills, and he may have learned something from facing Spofforth a couple of years before.

After their disappointments the previous year, 1881 saw Llandovery College drawn in the Challenge Cup against a new entrant, Aberdare United, from the northern end of the Glamorgan valleys. Once again the tie was played on neutral ground at Swansea, where Aberdare managed just 38 and 29 with Lewis taking three wickets in the first innings and seven in the second. He was run out for just four, but his boys took the total to 72 and set up an innings victory.

The match report in Swansea's new daily paper, the *Cambria Daily Leader*, also contained a glowing tribute to Lewis:

> Their best all round man, C.P.Lewis, did not meet with the success anticipated as he became a victim, when he had scored 4, to a very frequent misfortune among cricketers, viz run out. Mr Lewis, it will be remembered, is an old Oxford man, and has had the distinguished cricketing honour of having played in the University match. In fact when he figured as one of the Oxford team, he was in that year their most reliable bowler. Consequently C.P.Lewis has been, in South Wales, a household cricketing word. Llandovery can well be thankful for having such a man in their team.

The second-round tie was also held on neutral soil at St. Helen's against Morriston, the metalworks town on the western outskirts of Swansea, and one of a growing number of working men's clubs coming into what had basically been a competition for teams dominated by public school old boys. Llandovery duly upheld the honour of the old school ties, scoring 169 with C.P.Lewis making 85 (some sources say 86) before Morriston made just 49.

Their next opponents were old rivals Christ College, Brecon. The arrangements for their annual inter-school match had prohibited masters from playing, but in the Cup they could play. Llandovery had the worst of a draw but, possibly because it was late in the summer, Brecon withdrew from the replay. Aided by this piece of good fortune, Llandovery took their place in the final at St. Helen's against the Swansea Working Men's Club. To reach the final for the second successive summer was something of a feather in C.P.Lewis' already quite sizeable cap, and although all of the other premier clubs had fallen by the wayside, they could not treat their opponents lightly, especially as they had the Gwynn brothers – W.H. ('Bill') Gwynn and brother David – who were two of the most capable young sportsmen in the town, half-backs for the Welsh rugby team, as well as talented cricketers.

It proved to be a memorable match for C.P.Lewis, who proceeded to take five wickets as the Swansea side were bustled out for just 31. The students then secured a first-innings lead of 27, before Bill Gwynn showed the sort of form with the bat that was later to attract the attention of the Glamorgan selectors and resulted in his appearance for the county side in the 1890s. He struck a resounding 58 before being clean bowled by Owen Jones. C.P. then filleted the lower order, leaving the scholars with a target of 93. They had a few scares *en route* to it, including the loss of their talismanic leader for just 19, but the other batsmen held their nerve and on the second afternoon, C.P.Lewis and his boys were able to celebrate their victory by four wickets, and cast aside the bad memories of their defeat to Cardiff the previous year. The scorecard, its bowling details long since missing, read as follows:

Swansea Working Men's Club

L.J.Harrop	b H.E.Lewis	0	run out	5
C. Farr	b H.E.Lewis	1	b C.P.Lewis	6
W.H.Gwynn	run out	10	b O.Jones	58
J.Doggett	b C.P.Lewis	11	b O.Jones	0
E.M.Jones	b C.P. Lewis	0	b O.Jones	0
G.F.Beavan	b C.P.Lewis	0	b C.P.Lewis	4
J.Scott	b H.E.Lewis	0	b C.P.Lewis	2
S.Caird	b C.P.Lewis	1	c H.E.Lewis b C.P.Lewis	8
G.Brooks	b H.E.Lewis	8	b C.P.Lewis	13
B.Williams	b C.P.Lewis	0	not out	0
D.Gwynn	not out	0	b O.Jones	0
Extras		0		18
Total		31		114

Llandovery College

D.S.Jones	c Beavan b E.M.Jones	9	b Caird	0
J.Carver	run out	0	c Brooks b Jones	11
A.T.Lewis	not out	12	b Jones	10
G.T.Evans	b Doggett	13	thrown out W.H.Gwynn	32
C.P.Lewis	c Doggett b Caird	6	c Doggett b Jones	19
A.E.Kempthorne	c D.Gwynn b E.M.Jones	6	b Harrop	12
O.Jones	b E.M.Jones	3	not out	6
F.C.Cornish	b E.M.Jones	0		
H.E.Lewis	b Harrop	0		
A.E.Lewis	run out	3		
T.H.Bayley	b Doggett	2		
Extras		4		3
Total		58	(for six wkts)	93

The South Wales club matches, for several years the high point of C.P.'s cricket season, seem to have been rather low-key affairs in 1881, perhaps because of poor weather, although *James Lillywhite's Cricketers' Annual* published the club's averages for the first time. C.P. captained the side against M.C.C. at Cardiff in early August, scoring 25* out of 69, batting at seven, in reply to the Londoners' first-innings 135, but the match scarcely progressed to a second innings. The London tour was down to two matches, the return match with M.C.C and the regular fixture with the Surrey Club and Ground side. At Lord's, South Wales were dismissed for 85 and 127 and were defeated by nine wickets. At The Oval, Surrey

side, but they still included Walter Read, Kingsmill Key, Bobby Abel and Ted Barratt, who between them eventually clocked up over 1,600 first-class matches. The Cardiff player William Morgan took eight for 80 in Surrey's first innings, his best return for the club. Barratt took nine wickets with his slow left-arm bowling and Surrey won by nine wickets.

The journey back home resulted in a change in form as Clifton were beaten in Cardiff by seven wickets. Lewis was in fine form with the ball, taking six wickets in the first innings and nine for 39,[23] bowling throughout in the visitors' second innings. But in 1882 Clifton were not the force that they had been when they hosted the first-ever South Wales Club match over twenty years before, with Gloucestershire's teacher/batsman Frank Townsend – the father and grandfather of Test cricketers – the only 'name' player. Lewis continued his good bowling form when M.C.C. visited Cardiff, claiming the scalp of their star batsman William Gunn in each innings – bowled for seven in the first, and caught by J.P.Jones for six in the second. But William Hearn made 96*, whilst J.T.D.Llewelyn, in a rare appearance for M.C.C., made 33 batting at number nine, before being bowled by his vice-captain Lewis. Lewis took eight for 67 in 33 overs in the first innings, with five of his victims first-class cricketers, and a further five off 42 overs in the second innings. He hit a half-century in his own side's second innings, but these huge efforts did not bring a Welsh victory as M.C.C. won by three wickets.

There was one new addition to the South Wales C.C. fixture list for 1882, as Wiltshire were introduced with matches at the Arms Park starting on 11 August, and at Marlborough College on 25 August. In Cardiff, Lewis batted at number three, scoring 45 and took five wickets, all bowled, as Wiltshire scored just 78. He then took two for 55 as they made 189 for seven in the second innings. In the return match, much reduced by rain, he took one for 27 and scored 34. The averages published in the red *Lillywhite* annual of 1883 later showed him as the club's leading run-scorer, with 211 at 23.44, and the leading wicket-taker, 37 (more than all the other bowlers combined) at 11.24. Lewis continued playing well after the South Wales club's fixture list was complete, appearing for the College in mid-September against Llandeilo.

---

23   This was his best innings return for the South Wales Club in an eleven-a-side match.

By 1883 Lewis had commenced his training to be a solicitor in Llandovery, so he could have been forgiven for having spent less time than usual preparing for the new season. But there was little sign of it in the early matches, starting with a game between Llandovery Town and the College, spread over two weekends as he made a 'superb' 169 not out. He also enjoyed himself with the ball a few weeks later against Morriston, a growing power in local cricket, largely through the efforts of the Thissen brothers (one of of whom, Dan, became an impressive wicket-keeper with the early Glamorgan side). Nevertheless, Morriston were bowled out for 49 and reduced to 29 for four by the end of play as Lewis took seven for 14 in the first innings, five bowled and two lbw.

Knighton came to Llandovery on a wet Monday in July, when 'the home team had the best of luck on a nasty day'. For Knighton, 'Cobden hit tremendously hard when the ball and ground were wet,' reported the local newspaper, but in the second innings, the fiery bowling of Lewis and Douglas Jones was too strong as the Town side won. For the visit to Stradey Park to play Llanelli, Lewis moved up the order and opened the batting. He had a good game, scoring 49 and then taking seven for 31 as the home team were bowled out for 88. It was intended to be a benefit match for professional Frank Cruze, a Nottinghamshire man who stayed in South Wales and later became a newsagent. There was little charity shown as the beneficiary was lbw to Lewis for nought!

Although their matches in London brought them prestige, the South Wales Club had not won at either Lord's or The Oval since 1876: quite often they were simply heavily outgunned. Perhaps not surprisingly therefore, 1883 saw the Club abandon their London tour for a visit instead to North Wales, where the game had been increasing in popularity during the second half of the nineteenth century. Fixtures had been tentatively agreed with M.C.C. and Surrey for matches at Lord's and The Oval, but these were scratched when an agreement was reached with Sydney Platt – a businessman and cricket nut, a species not unknown even in the twenty-first century – who organised country-house matches on his Bryn-y-neuadd estate at Llanfairfechan, overlooking Anglesey and the Menai Straits. Platt was a friend of A.N.Hornby[24] who

---

24   Hornby, aged 36 in 1883, had been Lancashire captain since 1880 and had played for Lord Harris' side in Australia in 1878/79 and in The Oval Test match of 1882. He had played in nine England rugby internationals and, like Platt, was a fox-hunting enthusiast.

regularly played in his best country-house matches. Platt was also well connected within M.C.C. and I Zingari, and he had many good friends in South Wales, including the Bancrofts of Swansea. William Bancroft (junior), who had coached C.P. when he was at Norton Lodge School, was later employed by Platt to play and coach at Bryn-y-neuadd in the 1880s.

Despite his enthusiasm for the game, Platt had not been impressed by the casual attitude to cricket in north Wales. 'This year my patience is at an end,' he said in 1880, 'owing to an unpardonable piece of carelessness on the part of [the Conwy] secretary, my eleven were kept waiting on the ground for more than two hours; nor did the match commence until some time after the arrival of the Conwy eleven, owing to a fight which took place between two of the club.'

In an attempt to rectify matters, Platt raised a Caernarvonshire eleven in 1882 for matches against sides representing Flintshire and Anglesey, whilst he also paid for three professionals to turn out for his so-called county eleven, as well as for the Bryn-y-neuadd team in country-house matches. There were complaints from local clubs about the way Platt called his side Caernarvonshire, especially as only two of Platt's team played for teams in the area. As a result, a group of representatives from these clubs followed Platt's lead and inaugurated a 'proper' county club, with a committee populated by local representatives – an outcome which pleased Platt as it significantly improved the organisation of the game in Caernarvonshire.

Bryn-y-neuadd had been built as a fake castle-cum-abbey for Platt's father. It later became a mental hospital, before being demolished in 1970 to make way for a new hospital. Through Platt's involvement it became something of a cricketing mecca in the late nineteenth century with the length of the Bryn-y-neuadd fixture list for 1883 showing Platt's immense enthusiasm for the game, and his wide range of contacts. In fact, their match with the South Wales Club was one of twelve two-day matches at Bryn-y-neuadd that summer, with the Somerset Rovers, Manchester Club and Ground (the then name for Lancashire's second eleven) and the Gentlemen of Leicestershire amongst the other visitors.

The visit by the South Wales Club began with a twelve-a-side contest against Platt's country-house side, styled Bryn-y-neuadd,

71

with Lewis opening the batting with the Cardiff industrialist Sir Joseph Spearman, who had helped to underwrite some of the costs incurred in visiting North Wales. After their first game at Llanfairfechan, the South Wales club went across the English border to Shrewsbury, where they played Shropshire who had been playing county and county-style matches for many years, as well as annual games with M.C.C. since 1879. Then they returned to Llanfairfechan for another game – the same teams, but a different title this time branded as South Wales *v* North Wales. The matches were all drawn, with South Wales holding the advantage in all three. The circumstances of these were no doubt most agreeable, but none of these opponents[25] had anywhere near the firepower of the M.C.C., Surrey or Sussex sides which had figured in the South Wales Club's previous tours: so there is a hint, perhaps, of a slipping ambition. Lewis' own contributions to the matches were modest; thirteen runs in three innings and five wickets.

Besides covering the costs of their visit to North Wales, Joseph Spearman was also the main backer for a 'Cardiff Week' at the Arms Park, comprising matches with M.C.C. and Platt's North Wales XI. The South Wales club hoped that this week would boost interest in their activities. It also confirmed that the powerbase within the South Wales C.C. had shifted firmly towards the Cardiff club, whilst those individuals from the Swansea club, and further west – including Lewis – started to wield far less influence. Had he not been so busily involved with his legal training, perhaps Lewis would have strongly lobbied for a week, or at least a game, at St. Helen's or Neath. But now it appears he was just happy to get an opportunity to turn out wherever he could with his old friends and acquaintances.

In the M.C.C. match, Lewis scored nought and nine as M.C.C. won after bowling out South Wales for just 39 in their second innings. Frank Hearne of Kent, who played for England and South Africa in nineteenth-century Tests at the Cape, took five wickets in the innings. Lewis, though, did claim seven wickets in the match, including one from a return catch from Hearne. He then took three wickets in the following match, against North Wales, before

---

25 None of the Bryn-y-Neuadd sides figured in first-class cricket: their best-known sportsman was Arthur Dunn, the amateur football international. Shropshire's side included four players who had by then (or later) made appearances in first-class cricket. The best known of these was George Kemp, who played for Cambridge University from 1885 to 1888 and intermittently for Lancashire from 1885 to 1892. He was later an M.P. and member of the House of Lords.

playing in an exhibition match when it finished, involving the same players in a different combination called East *v* West Wales. He played for the West in this match, scoring 16 and 50 and taking seven wickets in an innings. Soon after he was again invited to play for Breconshire as they met Monmouthshire in Newport. He was out for 0 in the first innings, but he made Monmouthshire pay with an unbeaten 131 in the second. There were also three wickets in each innings.

Lewis also accepted invitations to guest for other teams during his summer vacations. He played for Cardiff as a guest against the Welsh Wanderers – a team originally put together by J.T.D. Llewelyn for 'missionary' work in the more remote parts of Wales – before joining the Wanderers team to meet Breconshire. He took three wickets and scored 9 and 80 – the latter probably when the match was dead, as Breconshire won on first innings with no time for a second innings conclusion.

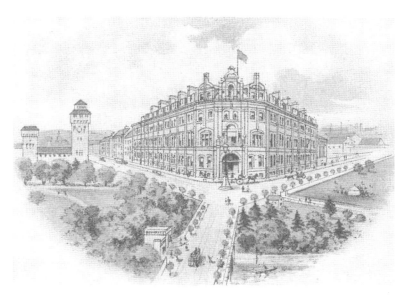

A 'carte de visite' for the Angel Hotel in Cardiff, showing the grounds of Cardiff Castle to the left and those of the Arms Park to the right. By the 1880s this area had become the epicentre of cricket in South Wales.

Chapter Eight

The Lone Full Back

Besides boasting a county cricket side which was, as we have seen, 'strong' by the local standards of the time, Breconshire's sportsmen were also the prime instigators behind the formation of a regional rugby team. In October 1875, when C.P.Lewis was still an Oxford undergraduate, two leading members of the Brecon Town rugby club, Major T. Conway Lloyd and H.W.Davies, formed the South Wales Football Club. The latter acted as secretary and treasurer, whilst the former was appointed president of the new organisation. Lloyd was also a fine cricketer and an influential member of the South Wales C.C. which was the inspiration for the new regional rugby club, run along similar lines 'with the intention of playing matches with the principal clubs in the West of England and neighbourhood.'

Newspaper announcement of the formation of the South Wales (Rugby) Football Club, in 1875. Although still an undergraduate at the time, and therefore understandably absent from the notice, many of those listed played both rugby and cricket alongside Lewis.

Like C.P. and his friends at Swansea, many of the gentlemen who played for the South Wales C.C. in their games at such grounds as Lord's and The Oval also turned out for the South Wales F.C. in their black and white jerseys during the 1870s against the strongest rugby teams from neighbouring parts of England, including Hereford, Clifton and a combined West of England side.

Amongst his colleagues in the South Wales rugby team was Swansea's cricket secretary, Charles Chambers, known as 'Zulu' by his friends. Chambers was a well-known rugby player, but cricket was clearly his first love as he kept close control of the followers of the oval ball, allowing no rugby at St. Helen's until November, and insisting the footballers were off the field by March in order for the grass to recover for the cricket season. The situation was reversed by the 1990s, when lush, rugby-length outfields on the Mumbles side of the ground kept county cricket scoring down to singles on one side, and where Championship matches always had to switch to Cardiff in September as the All-Whites would be in occupation.

It was measure of his standing within the rugby world, as well as his athletic abilities, that C.P. captained the South Wales side in many of these games. Given the strong overlap between cricket and rugby personnel, it was presumably quite natural for the participants from the Club to be led in their rugby-playing activities by the dynamic and skilful Lewis, who helped the winter game secure a toehold in the region.

His commitments at Oxford meant that, at first, he was just an enthusiastic supporter of the South Wales Football Club, playing from 1876 until 1882 against the likes of Clifton, Hereford, Gloucestershire, Old Leysians and Old Monmouthians.[26] However, in October 1878, he was appointed, as a representative of Llandovery College, to the Club's match committee, serving for the next few years alongside other eminent players including Raoul Foa, the captain of the Cardiff club, plus representatives from the thriving clubs at Newport and Swansea. It may have been no coincidence that following his appointment, the Club's fixture list broadened to include games with teams further away from Severnside.

---

26   For example, Lewis was in the South Wales side in 1876, when they played Clifton at Cardiff and Hereford at Hereford. In that same year, Gloucestershire won a match against South Wales at the Spa Ground in Gloucester, with Lewis captain and full-back for the visitors.

Indeed, by 1879 matches were scheduled to take place against a West of Scotland fifteen and a South of Ireland team. A few days before the contest with the Scottish side at Newport, the ambitious Welshmen had to cancel their first quasi-international game as the Scottish officials telegrammed to say that they were unable to send down a full team. However, later in the year the game against the Irish side went ahead, with C.P. contributing to the comprehensive victory, with *The South Wales Daily News* reporting how 'Lewis rendered invaluable service as a back, his kicking was clean and very effective.'

Some of Lewis' early appearances in the black and white shirts of the South Wales club had seen him play in the forwards. As in his early days with the Swansea club, Lewis was one of the Welsh forwards when the Clifton club visited Newport, in January 1878. His good friend T.B.Jones, who was the captain of the Abergavenny rugby club, was chosen as full-back for the South Wales side in what ended up as an acrimonious encounter, with the game ending in a draw after disputes over one of the conversions kicked by the Clifton team.

When he started to play regularly as a master at Llandovery College, C.P.'s playing position switched from the forwards to the backs. No doubt he found it easier to coach (and direct) his pupils by standing outside the scrum, rather than being in the hurly-burly of a maul, which in those days often involved far more of the fifteen team members than it does in twenty-first century rugby. His running skills were also put to good use in this new position, as evidenced in the match against Swansea on the College sports field at the end of October 1877, when he made several strong runs from his new position at full-back. 'The superior play of the boys soon began to tell,' wrote the *Western Mail*'s correspondent, 'Mr C.P.Lewis got the ball and from the centre of the ground, by one of the most brilliant runs seen on the field, ran through the visitors and obtained [another] try.'

His strong bursts became a key tactic in the College's play, and helped to win several games – an example being the contest the following year against Cowbridge Grammar School at St. Helen's, when he made a series of fine runs through the Cowbridge defence. One of these saw him brought to earth just short of the try-line, but the Llandovery forwards were in close support and drove over the line for a match-winning score. When weather conditions were wet, or the turf was saturated and less conducive to running rugby, this tactic was modified with C.P. playing at half-back – or scrum-half in modern terminology – as the Llandovery students hoped their star master would pick up the ball from the forwards and bulldoze his way through the opponents in the muddy conditions.

Through his efforts, C.P. established the College as a stronghold in the Welsh rugby scene, building on the pioneering work of W.P.Whittington back in the 1860s. When, at the end of his student days, Lewis returned to the College, their fixture list included fixtures against Llandovery Town; Christ College, Brecon; St. David's College, Lampeter; and an Old Boys fifteen. Within a few years, the fixture list had expanded to include games against several of the major clubs, with C.P. revelling in the off-field arrangements, and as one ex-pupil reminisced, 'when we played games some distance from Llandovery, we often travelled in an enlarged waggonette driven by C.P.Lewis and were accompanied by a band of enthusiastic supporters'.

Through his influence, Llandovery College also participated in the South Wales Football Challenge Cup which the South Wales Club launched at a meeting at the Cardiff Arms Hotel in October 1877. The College were amongst the eighteen founder members in the competition for the cup,[27] with the influence of these educational centres in the spread of rugby fever and the adoption of the game as the national sport of Wales clearly evident from the presence of the Grammar Schools from Monmouth, Cowbridge and Carmarthen, besides St. David's College, Lampeter alongside Llandovery College in the first-round draw, against leading town clubs including Cardiff, Merthyr, Brecon, Llanelli, Newport, Neath and Swansea. Llandovery practised at the start of the season with a match against a 'Carmarthenshire Rovers' team, a side probably composed mainly of Old Boys from the school. Seemingly they had an easy draw in that first year, against the Glamorgan 10th Rifle Volunteers (Cardiff), which was played at Swansea. After helping to defeat Merthyr in the second round, C.P. led the College in the semi-final at Brecon, where they lost to Newport, the eventual winners of the Cup, by two goals to nil.

The competition proved to be a huge success. David Smith and Gareth Williams, in their neatly titled 1981 book, *Fields of Praise,*

---

27   The trophy was valued at fifty guineas in 1877, equivalent to £3,700 in 2009 money, so it was never intended to be minor competition.

have commented how the Challenge Cup 'became the pivot around which early Welsh rugby revolved. It played a formative role in the emergence of Welsh Rugby and in its growth as a spectator sport. It generated intense local rivalry and brought excitement and spectacle into the routine lives of congested, industrial towns. It also raised the standard of football played.'

The success though came at a cost, with many bitter disputes between the participating clubs and allegations of 'illegal' players being hired, as clubs flouted the 'twelve-mile' rule over eligibility. The latter did not affect Llandovery College, but C.P. believed strongly that player hiring was wrong, and on several occasions, he contacted the Press to express his anger. The College's games however were not immune from other problems and sometimes they were affected by the overly partisan behaviour of the crowds. The match report of their contest at Carmarthen in 1881 said, of the home side's supporters, that 'the conduct of the mob was disgraceful.'

There were often rows about alleged bias in the refereeing, as in Llandovery College's match in November 1878 against St. David's College, Lampeter. It proved to be quite a heated affair with disputes over the legality of some of the tries and conversions kicked by the Lampeter side, and after one protracted exchange in the second half, C.P. led the Llandovery side off the pitch, causing the game to finish early. Nothing though was mentioned about these disputes, or the abrupt end, in the match report in the *Western Mail,* submitted by presumably someone with strong Lampeter connections. This omission infuriated C.P. who duly wrote to the newspaper, and had his letter published a few days later, with his comments putting the record straight: 'Nothing is said about the try and goal which Llandovery claim, but which Lampeter dispute, and as the latter would not kick off from half-way after the goal, the game was brought to an abrupt conclusion quarter of an hour before the final whistle.'

Such disputes and arguments were the undoing of the South Wales Football Challenge Cup, but in part, some of the friction and regional rivalries were the South Wales Football Club's own making. In September 1880, for instance, they decided to divide the contesting clubs into eastern and western districts, thereby ensuring a potentially fractious East *v* West final each year. As far as the Llandovery students were concerned, the change brought about a contest with the Neath club, which had been formed in

1871 by a group of the town's young professional men, including Lewis Kempthorne, an Old Llandoverian, who like C.P. had picked up the rugby 'bug' from W.P.Whittington. In fact, the latter's brother, Tom, was their first captain and played for Scotland in 1873 when a student in Edinburgh.

However, the College withdrew from the contest with Neath in 1881, largely because of the increasing competitiveness of the matches which sometimes contradicted Lewis' more Corinthian ideals, as clearly evidenced in the rumpus with St. David's College, Lampeter. When Llandovery College played a number of clubs in the early 1880s, the College side which took the field included several Old Boys in its line-up, suggesting that there was a need for more world-wise and robust young men, rather than 'callow and innocent youths' in these heated and quite physical contests. Indeed, when the Llandovery College XV played St. David's, Lampeter in 1882, C.P. played in a side containing no fewer than six current or future Welsh internationals, with the College's line-up including Edward Alexander, Edward Bishop, Thomas Judson, Alfred Mathews and Rowland Thomas, some of whom, in addition, subsequently played Minor Counties cricket for Carmarthenshire.

In 1879 the South Wales Football Club metamorphosed into the South Wales Football Union, and the seeds had been sown for the creation of a body which would oversee the organisation of rugby in the region. Once again, C.P. and his good friend J.T.D.Llewelyn were in the vanguard of developments, with C.P. as the captain of the South Wales side, and J.T.D. the President of the Union and, in the words of a letter to the Union's secretary, 'eager to do what he could to further the effectiveness of South Wales sports.'

However, there were others who were equally eager to form a Wales side and, through Richard Mullock of the Newport rugby club, a match was arranged at Blackheath against England on 19 February 1881. It is regarded now by rugby historians as the first Welsh international: at the time, though, there were heated discussions about how representative the Welsh side was. C.P. may have been amongst the early dissenters, and as a staunch member of the South Wales Club, he might have from the outset not seen eye to eye with Mullock, and may have rejected an invitation to play for what he regarded as a renegade outfit. What is known for certain is that Lewis' name never appeared on any of the team lists published before the game.

The problems, though, were not over by the time the Welsh players finally arrived to change at a nearby pub prior to the game at Blackheath. They found two of their chosen players had not arrived, so a couple of the named reserves, both University players, were drafted into the starting line-up.[28] One of the missing players was J.E.Brooks of Pontypridd and he later claimed that 'there was no organization or committee to select players for the matches organised by Mullock. All that would happen was that some individual would have a conversation with you, take your name and address and pass on. That happened to me after I had played for Pontypridd at Sophia Gardens. It was mentioned to me that Treharne and I had been chosen to play for Wales against England. I had no definite instructions from anyone to play in that match, but I heard afterwards that I had been expected to play.' However, recent research has shown that Brooks' name never appeared on any of the official team-lists, and rugby historians believe that Brooks' claims may have held water in earlier times, especially with other teams, but they are far more sceptical about the Wales-England match, debunking what appears like a good story, but in essence, was just unfounded tittle-tattle.

Llandovery's fly-half, Aneurin Rees, did play, but was injured early on. Wales, with nine forwards, were swamped by England's ten-strong pack, and England got a 'ridiculously easy' victory by eight goals and six unconverted tries to nil – 86 points to nil under the twenty-first century scoring system – a sporting disaster which had an immediate benefit as it prompted the officials of the leading Welsh clubs to convene a meeting on 12 March 1881 at the Castle Hotel, Neath to establish a Welsh Rugby Football Union which would organise rugby in the principality, and organise properly a Welsh national side to play internationals against England, Scotland and Ireland. C.P. attended as Llandovery College's representative and was no doubt pleased to mingle with many of his friends from the South Wales Club. He was probably even more delighted when the assembled mass decided that the members of the Club should retain their importance in the new oragnisation, with Chambers becoming the inaugural President, succeeded in 1885 by J.T.D.Llewelyn, whilst C.P.Lewis was appointed as one of two vice-presidents.

---

28 *The Times* reporter at the match commented rather soberly: '... it is probable, had the decision of the contest been possible at an earlier period, the Welsh executive would have had more material at their command.'

Evidently, the links between cricket and early Welsh rugby were exceptionally close as, in September 1881, C.P. was invited to play for a Newport and District XXII against an All England Eleven which included W.G.Grace. Alongside Lewis in the Newport side were Newport cricketers George Harding, Frank Purdon and Charles Newman, all of whom were prominent rugby players – in fact, only four months later, all four were members of the Welsh fifteen which defeated Ireland. Before then, the four cricketers played together in a Welsh side against the North of England. Although no caps were awarded, this was an important match for Wales as they gave a spirited performance that persuaded England to re-instate them to a full international fixture the following season.

Lewis' appointment as a vice-president of the Welsh Rugby Union reflected his high standing amongst sporting circles, and stemmed from the fact that he had been the captain of the South Wales side: a position which he maintained when he made his Welsh rugby debut on 28 January 1882, as the national side – now selected in a more formal and organised way – played Ireland at Lansdowne Road, Dublin.

Not surprisingly, there were eleven changes from the team that Mullock had chosen for the inaugural international at Blackheath. C.P.'s partner at full-back was S.S. ('Sam') Clark, a solicitor from Neath, who had acted as the secretary of the South Wales Rugby Football Union, besides being a leading cricketer with the town club and a member of M.C.C. At the time the practice was to have two full-backs, a generally defensive arrangement, with one man gathering back to feed the other who either kicked the ball away, or ran up field. Given Lewis' athletic abilities, he must have relished the prospect of the latter role, as well as being the side's goal-kicker. However, he managed to convert only two of the four Welsh tries in a match in which Ireland did not get on the scoreboard. They had continuous disputes with the referee, who unfortunately was the secretary of the Welsh Rugby Union; two Irish players walked off in protest, and two others were injured, so that Ireland finished with eleven men on the field. Lewis, though, was very happy, as he duly went down in the annals of Welsh sport as the first man to lead a Welsh rugby side to victory in an international match.

Wales' first-ever home match was against England at St. Helen's, Swansea on a rainy and blustery day, 'disagreeable' according to *The Times* reporter, in mid-December 1882. C.P. played in the

Lewis, third from the right in the middle row, was captain of this Welsh side which defeated Ireland at Lansdowne Road, Dublin in June 1882, the Principality's first rugby win.

scarlet jersey of Wales alongside D.H.Bowen, a Llanelli schoolteacher, as full-backs. The side also included David Gwynn, the star cricketer from Swansea Working Men's club, and Thomas Judson, the science master at Llandovery College, who made his Welsh debut as one of the forwards. He made only one subsequent appearance before moving to teach at Highgate School in 1883. Although not winning any further Welsh caps, Judson retained his involvement in rugby, playing for London Welsh and serving as their treasurer. His close friendship with C.P. no doubt explains why Lewis played for London Welsh a few years later when he was 'up in town' as part of his training as a solicitor.

The selection of the two Llandovery masters for the match against England may well have been the result of their outstanding play the previous week when the College – to C.P.'s delight – defeated Swansea. However, the international saw England win by two goals and four tries to nil, as the Welsh side – so used to a forwards-dominated style with mauls and rucks – were run off their feet by a new system of three-quarters play, led by the powerful running wing Gregory Wade of Richmond.

In the words of the *South Wales Daily News*, 'the passing of the [English] backs was brilliant in the extreme and the Welshmen appeared quite undone. The home team were all of a heap defending their goal as every opening was invaded. Every weak point was tested by the Englishmen,[29] and but for a short time, the Welshmen managed to keep them back.' C.P. valiantly launched some counter-attacks, but as the newspaper also reported 'Lewis got a run but soon lost the ball and 'ere long, the wonderful passing of the visitors proved too much for the home side.'

In January of that season Wales went to Raeburn Place, Edinburgh to play Scotland. This was a game staged on a frozen pitch, and one which saw Lewis became the first Welsh player to play at full-back on his own. It was also a match which saw the Welsh forwards, led by the tall Tom Clapp – another Newport cricketer – manage one move which swept the length of the field and enabled Tom Judson to score a try which Lewis adroitly converted. But the Scots proved too powerful, scoring three converted tries. In fact, it might have been more had it not been for some spirited tackling by Lewis when the burly Scots forwards launched a series of attacks on the Welsh line.

The next international was nearly a year later, on 5 January 1884, against England in Leeds, at the St. John's Ground in Cardigan Fields. Lewis was replaced as captain by Charles Newman of Newport for the match, which was played in heavy rain and on already saturated turf, but he did manage to convert the only Welsh try of the match, scored by the Oxford Blue and Bangor cricketer, Charles Allen, after a 'grand dash and kick over the English line'. England however crossed the try-line three times and, as in the match against Scotland, Lewis' spirited defence helped to keep the score down, whilst his accurate drop-kicks launched several counter-attacks. Indeed, the correspondent of *The South Wales Daily News* believed that 'praise should be given to the full-back Lewis who defended exceedingly well.'

C.P. kept his place in the side the following week and regained the captaincy when Scotland visited Newport – a game which attracted a crowd of around 7,000, with Wales starting as pre-match favourites. However, the match at Rodney Parade saw Scotland secure a comprehensive victory in what proved to be C.P.'s final appearance in a Welsh jersey. His strong tackling was to the fore again, but Wales needed more attacking options in the backs, and

---

29   The English fifteen included seven Oxford University players, and one from
      Cambridge, indicating the continuing prominence of students at the national
      level of sport.

when C.P. tried to launch an attack, he was soon brought to earth by the enthusiastic Scots, often to the displeasure of the partisan crowd who vented their feelings with loud jeers. The correspondent of the *Western Mail* was also critical, reporting that 'Lewis played well at back, but should have run less and punted sooner.'

Welsh supporters at one of C.P.'s rugby internationals.

It was clear to the Welsh selectors that a faster runner was needed at full-back, so for the match against Ireland in April 1884, Lewis was replaced at full-back by T.M. ('Tom') Barlow, a prominent solicitor and amateur sportsman. Born and educated in Lancashire, Barlow had moved to Cardiff in 1880 to train as a solicitor, having already turned down an offer to play cricket for Gloucestershire. As well as being a fine rugby player, he was a free-scoring batsman who had played alongside C.P.Lewis for the South Wales C.C. on their North Wales tour in 1883.

However, Barlow's international rugby career was a brief one, as he sustained a bad knee injury, precipitated by a series of heavy tackles, and his appearance against Ireland was his sole cap. Some thought that Lewis would return in January 1885 for the match with England, but by this time, the legendary Arthur Gould of Newport – another swift and skilful runner – had come on the scene, and the match with England at Swansea launched the career of a player described by rugby historians as 'the man who put Wales on the rugby map', and the man who captained Wales to their first Triple Crown.

Gould was also so good that the Welsh Rugby Union later bent the amateur rules and allowed him to keep a house donated by public subscription. An outstanding all-round sportsman, and one of six talented sporting brothers, Gould also played cricket for Monmouthshire between 1897 and 1903,[30] and as far as rugby was concerned, he certainly had more finesse in attack than Lewis, with

---

30   An amateur middle-order batsman, Gould played eight matches in the Minor Counties Championship for Monmouthshire from 1897 to 1903, scoring 112 runs at 10.18, and taking three catches.

an ability to dodge, swerve and side-step past opponents, rather than attempting just to bulldoze his way through, or, as C.P. also tried, 'to chip and chase'. He was also a sound tackler and a fine kicker, with a remarkably strong drop-kick.

Gould went on to win 27 caps for Wales as Lewis bowed out of the international arena to cat-calls at Newport, and the jibes about the team's poor performance were an inauspicious end to a distinguished rugby-playing career which had been ignited by the inspirational encouragement of W.P.Whittington on the playing fields of Llandovery. He subsequently participated in the next international against England at Swansea in January 1885, but this time he was the match referee,[31] no doubt drawing on his experiences of overseeing games at Llandovery College.

This was his last 'appearance' in a top-flight match, but for the next few years, C.P. was still held in very high regard in rugby circles. He was re-elected on an annual basis as a vice-president to the Welsh Rugby Union until 1890 – a post which reflected his services to Welsh rugby as well as an ability to chair meetings, as he did with the South Wales Cricket Club. By 1890, the Welsh Rugby Union began electing vice-presidents from representatives of the various districts within the Union, and it was from this time that C.P.'s direct involvement with rugby came to an end.

---

31   There was no special refereeing 'cadre' at the time and internationals were often refereed by administrators of the organisations involved.

Chapter Nine
South Wales Cricket Club: A Dream Dies

By the time that C.P. bowed out of international rugby, he had decided to switch careers, handing in his resignation in 1883 to the Warden of Llandovery College and entering the solicitor's practice of his good friend and fellow Llandovery cricketer, Charles Bishop. As we have seen in Chapter Four, Bishop had been instrumental in forming the Carmarthenshire club in the 1860s. C.P.'s decision to change career may well have been the result of mixing with the kind of people who frequented county matches and country-house games.

The precocious student-sportsman was by now a mature man of thirty, who had perhaps come to realize that he wanted to do more than just teaching and coaching youngsters. His possession of a pass rather than an honours degree perhaps limited his promotion prospects. Indeed, many of his sporting contemporaries now had very respectable jobs in a range of professions. Although schoolmasters were held in high regard by some, the time had therefore come for him to leave Llandovery College once and for all. He'd achieved much for his pupils – especially on the sports field – but now it was time for Lewis to put himself first, and carve out a niche away from academia. He'd seen a school cricketing generation reach maturity, too, and may have preferred fresh challenges to doing it all again. It wasn't an acrimonious split as he continued to live near the College and in his spare time also helped coach some of the youngsters. A sports day programme from October, 1884 also names him as guest 'starter' for the sprints, and he carried on coaching cricket for some years until the College engaged a professional, Walter Attewell,[32] a cousin of William, the Nottinghamshire and England cricketer.

But with his training in London taking up more and more of his time – his pass degree had involved no legal studies and so did not provide him with a short cut to a professional qualification – C.P.'s

---

32   The surviving records do not credit him with a first name, but Walter coached at several schools during his career.

appearances at Llandovery College started to decline. New opportunities came his way in the Home Counties, including playing rugby for Rosslyn Park and London Welsh, alongside other Welshmen who worked up in town. Whilst in London, he was also able to develop further his already impressive list of contacts in the social and political world, and a number of acquaintances who were to stand him in good stead in the course of the next few decades as he started to wind down his sporting activities.

Despite his new commitments in the legal world, Lewis continued to find plenty of time to play cricket, and he still led the South Wales C.C. in their fixtures in 1884, besides chairing the club's annual general meeting on 10 April at the Mackworth Hotel in Swansea. The season began in June with the annual trial match, but there were signs that the trainee solicitor had slightly lost some of his speed and agility running between the wickets as he was run out, albeit for 31 and 41, in each innings. Nevertheless, he was still an explosive bowler, completing a match haul of twelve wickets in the trial game.

Later in the summer, Lewis, together with his good friend and club teammate Douglas Jones, travelled up to London for the annual tour. Jones was the other class player of the Llandovery side. In his early days he played a lot of country-house cricket in Wales and the Marches but his cricket became less as his local government career advanced. By this time Jones was Deputy Clerk – we'd say Deputy Chief Executive these days – to the first Carmarthenshire County Council, a post he held until 1900. From then, he was a Registrar – or a minor judge – at Llandovery County Court, dealing with small civil cases, before becoming clerk to Llandovery's Poor Law Guardians and to the Rural District Council, which ran the town and its rural surrounds. In fact, it may well have been Jones who first suggested to Lewis that he move into the legal world and train as a solicitor.

On the 1884 London tour, Lewis scored 75 and took two wickets against M.C.C. at Lord's, besides appearing at The Oval and also at Wormwood Scrubs against the local club, Kensington Park, who had been added to the tour itinerary. By including professionals in their number for the first time – Johnny Donovan of Cardiff took eleven wickets at Lord's, for example – South Wales became more convincing opponents. They forced M.C.C. to follow on at Lord's and ran up a total of 348 against Kensington Park.

For their return visit to the Arms Park later in August, M.C.C. sent down another strong eleven with three professionals from Nottinghamshire who later won England Test caps – the medium-pace bowler William Attewell, all-rounder Wilfred Flowers, and the elegant middle-order bat William Gunn. It wasn't a great game for South Wales. They were bundled out for 72 in the first innings by Flowers' eight-wicket return and in the second for only 46, courtesy of Attewell's eight-wicket analysis, for only twelve runs off nineteen overs. Lewis, though, did get top score for the home side, a modest 23.

Having left Llandovery College, it was the town's cricket club which increasingly grew in importance in Lewis' life. During the 1880s, he duly acted as their treasurer, whilst Douglas Jones served as secretary. These were boom years for the town club, with its colours of chocolate and blue, and it grew in importance as Lewis gave it his full attention. Llandovery teams no longer took part in the Challenge Cup competition, which had started to decline in importance. The club were able to employ the services of various professionals – a bowler called Edwards fulfilled this role in 1883, followed by another called Shaw in 1884 and then another called Prytherch, a curious coincidence, from 1885 until 1888. C.P. also acted as a benefactor to the club's less affluent members, giving generous donations towards their kit and clothing.

With such prominent cricketers as Lewis and Jones in their ranks, Llandovery Town C.C., playing for the most part in one-day matches, enjoyed a very successful period and recorded many fine victories. For example, in 1884 Jones made a magnificent 114 in the Town *v* Gown match, and also collected seven wickets. Later that summer, Lewis' bowling decimated the batting of the Builth Wells club, from another droving town in mid-Wales. Llandovery scored 113, then bowled Builth out for 29 and 44, with Lewis returning figures of eight for 4 and six for 10, with his second innings analysis including four bowled in successive balls. A couple of days later Llandovery played Swansea and Lewis scored 112. Detailed records still exist for quite a few of Llandovery's matches in the seven years 1883 to 1889 and these show that he scored 24 fifties in those matches, the highest being his 169* *v* Llandovery College in 1883, and took thirty-five five-wicket hauls, one of the best being eight for 19 at Llandeilo in the same year. No doubt there were other games whose details have been lost.

He still found time to play for the South Wales C.C. in 1885, whose activities now included home and away matches with Worcestershire, still almost a decade short of the Foster family's influence, but there was no cricket week in Cardiff, only a visit to the coal metropolis by M.C.C. The London tour comprised just two matches, with Surrey and M.C.C.: he enjoyed modest success on the tour, scoring 22 and 30 at number five in the match at The Oval, before scoring 48 and taking three wickets at Lord's.

It proved to be his last full year of activities with the South Wales club as, at the 1886 annual general meeting, he stood down from both the match committee and the vice-captaincy. For once, he didn't even attend the annual meeting, with J.P.Jones being elected in his place. In his absence he was re-elected to the match committee, but later wrote stating his inability to accept the office. There was further evidence as well that he was clearly disenchanted with the organisation of the club, given his submission of a notice of motion 'that the South Wales Challenge Cup be discontinued'. It was, however, ruled out-of-order because it had not been submitted early enough to go out with the agendas. The big clubs had begun to abandon the Cup, no doubt because of the bad behaviour by players and crowds, and it was becoming more of a competition for newer and lesser clubs.

Lewis in a South Wales club cap in about 1886

The 1886 season began without Lewis appearing in the South Wales annual trial, held in Newport, although he still went to Lord's to play against M.C.C., where he made 43 and 81 at number six, and failed to take a wicket. It proved to be his, and the South Wales Club's last appearance at headquarters. They also played a nostalgic farewell match at Prince's, against the Surrey Club and Ground side. The Surrey side included three players who in their time played Test cricket, plus Robert Henderson, a *Wisden* 'Cricketer of the Year' in 1890 and they duly won by eight wickets. Lewis batted at second wicket down, scoring 0 and 33, and took two for 22 in the first innings. By the 1886 annual general meeting, held at the Angel Hotel in Cardiff, most of the cricket clubs in the region seemed to have come round to Lewis' point of view that the Challenge Cup served little purpose. The leading clubs had gradually abandoned it after years of acrimonious contest, bad behaviour from players and crowds, and in its closing years, the competition was dominated by newer and junior clubs seeking prestige. It was therefore decided not only to discontinue the competition, but the club as well, with South Wales' leading cricketers expected to go off and form individual county clubs. As with so many club cricket leaders, Lewis would have done a lot of the work himself, and as a mark of thanks, it was also resolved to present the now-defunct cup to Lewis 'as a token of esteem and in recognition of the services rendered by him to South Wales cricket.' It was perhaps the grandest-ever leaving gift presented to a cricket official in Wales.

These decisions at the 1886 meeting also symbolised a seismic shift in the thinking of the hierarchy of the South Wales C.C., now led by J.P.Jones and supported by a series of influential figures in south-east Wales – hence the decision to hold the meeting in Cardiff rather than in Swansea. The *mantra* of the new committee was to create county teams representing Wales, and with the English County Championship having flourished in the 1880s, there was clearly a mood to create *similar* teams representing the counties of South Wales. At this stage it was by no means inevitable that Glamorgan would come to be Wales' only first-class representative, though with hindsight we can see they had a majority of the 'premier' clubs.

J.P.Jones also represented the dynamism and energy of the emerging middle-classes of urban Wales, whereas Lewis and other senior members of the club represented the squirearchy and the gentry who had first formed the South Wales club back in 1859. The mood for change was also assisted by nationalistic feelings which had swept, like a tidal wave, across the teeming industrial centres of the region during the 1880s. It was in these years that the National Eisteddfod Society become inaugurated to co-ordinate the cultural and artistic affairs, as well as a University College of South Wales and Monmouthshire. 1881 had seen the creation of the Welsh Rugby Union, and now five years or so later, it was time for cricket to change, and for the South Wales C.C. to move forward.

In order for this to happen, a line had to be drawn under the past, so at the 1886 annual meeting, J.P.Jones proposed dissolving the South Wales Club and asking the managing committee to oversee the formation of county sides. This was agreed upon and Jones soon made arrangements for a series of matches in 1886 at Newport, the Arms Park and Llanelli between a Glamorgan side and the Rest of South Wales. Nothing eventually came of the games at either Cardiff and no scorecard survives from Llanelli, but Jones was able to lead a Glamorgan eleven into the field at Newport against an eighteen of South Wales – a match which symbolized this change to the basic structure of cricket in the region and the end of C.P.'s role at the forefront of sporting developments.

Since his brief five-match stretch in first-class cricket at Oxford, C.P.Lewis had had thirteen seasons in the highest class of club cricket, and it seemed an appropriate time for him to fade from the scene. When South Wales played their final match, at Swansea on 9 and 10 August, against M.C.C., who had brought down six first-class cricketers in their side, he did not play, even though his friend J.T.D.Llewelyn turned out for the visitors. He wasn't even in the Llandovery team which played Swansea at Llandovery, for long an important match, at the end of August. By now, he had been elected to Llandovery Town Council[33] and was taking work and civic affairs seriously. His reputation as a trustworthy local solicitor was growing, as was his waistline.

Errant headgear.
Two of C.P.'s cricket caps - left
is South Wales C.C. and right
Carmarthenshire C.C.C. - which
were found in a Llandovery
bank in the 1990s.
Lewis seems to have had a
penchant for hooped caps.

---

33   As an independent. Political parties were very rare in local government at that time, although no doubt he formed 'political' alliances of various kinds during his time as a local authority member. He became an alderman in 1899 – an appointed, rather than an elected member of the Council – eventually retiring in 1920.

Chapter Ten
Sporting Solicitor

Within eighteen months of the South Wales C.C. being wound up, Glamorgan County Cricket Club was formed, to become the flag-bearer of county cricket in the Principality. A few years later Monmouthshire followed suit, but despite occasional matches by Breconshire, Radnorshire and Pembrokeshire, the ideal of a series of Welsh county clubs stalled. Many of the leading representatives from the old organisation were instrumental in the creation of the new Glamorgan county club. J.T.D.Llewelyn was the instigator behind the meeting convened at the Angel Hotel in early July 1888, at which Glamorgan were formed following several weeks of canvassing by the two leading officials from the South Wales club – J.P. Jones of Cardiff C.C. and C.C.Chambers of Swansea C.C. – to secure the support of the leading clubs in the West and East.

Indeed, the attendance list at that meeting in the plush Cardiff hotel, opposite the Arms Park, read like a Who's Who of Welsh cricket, with the exception of C.P.Lewis, who did not attend and played no role in the Glamorgan club. His absence was rather surprising, given the fact that he was still in decent form as a cricketer, and was only in his mid-thirties. His massive involvement with the South Wales Club for many years also meant that he had a plethora of contacts both inside and outside Wales which could have only been beneficial to the fledgling county club.

But it would appear that Lewis did not exactly see eye-to-eye with J.P.Jones, after so many years as Llewelyn's right-hand man with the South Wales Club. When South Wales played their final match against M.C.C. at Swansea, as we have seen, Lewis didn't play, but perhaps we shouldn't read too much into this as C.P. was starting to play less cricket. As we have said, he had been elected to Llandovery Town Council, and he was clearly taking his legal work and civic affairs seriously, and putting his energies to community use.

As to his activities as a lawyer, there are no dramatic court cases on record involving Lewis, and he appears to have been a jobbing country solicitor, handling conveyancing, dealing with wills, financial affairs, and appearances at the local magistrates' court, allowing him to build even further his list of contacts and acquaintances. He duly qualified as a solicitor in January 1887 and appears in the Law Lists of the time, in the same practice as Charles Bishop, styled in the early days as Snow, Snow and Fox, a splendidly lawyerly title, one of three or four small solicitors' practices in Llandovery. It seems likely that his sociability enabled the practice to grow, and having spent so much of his time in the Llandovery area, the chance of rising to the top of local society, and being a really big fish in a small pool, now seems to have appealed to him greatly. By now, he probably had less appetite for getting involved in a new county club, with its focus some distance away from Llandovery. The peace and quiet of the country town and its rural surroundings probably meant more to him than the cut-and-thrust of the rapidly expanding industrial settlement at the mouth of the River Taff, never mind having to associate with the urban bourgeoisie such as J.P.Jones.

Had he particularly wanted to, Lewis might have commanded a place in the Glamorgan side – he might even have been its captain – as he remained an effective performer for several years in club cricket in West Wales, as well as playing for M.C.C. in various matches during his time off from his solicitor's practice. With his West Wales connections, though, it is unlikely he would have felt any close affinity with Glamorgan. He played for Llandovery against Llanelli in August 1887, scoring 41 at number three, and sharing a productive partnership with Douglas Jones, who made 90. Lewis took five wickets, having the Llanelli and Wales fly-half J.G. 'Johnny Bach' Lewis – we should think of him as the Stephen Jones or Phil Bennett of his day – caught by Jones for nine.

The growing strength of adult cricket over the schoolboy game can be seen in 1888, when Llandovery Town ran up 334 for three against the College, D.T.M.Jones making 158 and C.P.Lewis 152 not out, the entire innings lasting just three and a quarter hours. Things had changed dramatically in ten years, including, in the previous year, the College ground being moved to its present location alongside the River Tywi, although the square was nearer the College end until a revamp just before World War Two. A pavilion was added in 1892, and it was that ground which was used for representative matches. The Town Club played elsewhere, probably alongside the Castle, on land now Llandovery's municipal park, where they still play. Until recent years the rugby side played there as well.

In 1889 Llandovery played at Swansea in July. Lewis made 0, but had three wickets, all bowled. The match was notable for an early appearance for Llandovery by F.E.Chapman, uncle of the Ashes winning captain of 1926, Percy, whose carefree attitudes owe much to the tradition his uncle and father tapped into at Llandovery in the 1890s. Frank Chapman was a master at the College from 1886 to 1896 and his brother, C.E., Percy's father, was a clergyman who followed him to the area. The club averages for that year appear in the red *Lillywhite* annual. Lewis, who was captain and secretary for the sixteen-match programme, was second in the batting averages, but heaviest scorer with 361 runs from 17 innings, and top of the bowling, with 71 wickets at an average of just 6.33.

Indeed, C.P. was still good enough to play for M.C.C. against county sides and other decent elevens. In fact, in 1890, now 37, C.P. accepted an invitation to play for M.C.C. against Glamorgan at Swansea: he might also have helped assemble the M.C.C. side, perhaps with the hope of settling a few old scores with J.P.Jones and others in the county hierarchy. The M.C.C. team included Edwin Powell, who played some cricket with Llandovery but had also been Llanelli full-back in a Challenge Cup rugby final, and Powell's brother Frank, a Welsh international centre and crisp middle-order bat.

He duly batted at number five but scored just 24 and one, and when it came to bowling, he failed to claim a wicket, though by now, he was more of a change bowler with his days as a 'strike' bowler way behind him. Nevertheless, M.C.C. got the upper hand against the Glamorgan amateurs, winning by three wickets 'after playing about half an hour over time by request of the captains.' The match at Swansea seems to have re-ignited his appetite to play at a higher level, as he also accepted an invitation to play for M.C.C. against Leicestershire at Lord's a fortnight later. However, he met with less success and was dismissed by A.D.Pougher for 3 and 5, and did not take a wicket.

He continued to enjoy much success at club level with the Llandovery Town side, whose fixture list by now included a pleasant sojourn to the seaside resort of Tenby. The two-day contest saw the latter make 84 and 69 whilst Llandovery amassed

213. Lewis took six wickets, three in each innings and five bowled. Against Brecon he scored 50 at number five, and took four wickets – again every one bowled.

By this time, there were other things which mattered to him, as in June 1892 he got married – at the ripe old age of 39 – to a locally-born lady called Elizabeth Walters. After their wedding, the happy couple went up to London and spent some of their honeymoon watching play at Lord's and socialising with many of C.P.'s friends and acquaintances. Lizzie herself was 47 at the time of their marriage, and for several years before, she had been living quite near him at Llandingat Cottage with her older sister Anne. She came from a well-to-do family, and with C.P. destined to be Mayor of Llandovery, Mrs Lewis may have been partly an apprentice mayoress. No doubt Lewis knew he was due to inherit the chairmanship of Llandovery Council in another couple of years, and a woman of quite mature years certainly fitted the bill as Mayoress. It is fashionable nowadays to write of the great influence of the women of great men in pre-equality times, but in truth we know very little of Elizabeth. It is unlikely she would have been a twentieth-century style cricket wife, coming down to the ground to make the teas. We suspect that would have been thought beneath the wives of the solid professional men of the Llandovery club, especially when maids were employed for that kind of thing!

After returning from his honeymoon, Lewis continued to play club cricket with some effect. In another match with Swansea he made 23 out of just 67, and also took two wickets. He gets a mention in the red *Lillywhite*, for hitting the stumps and sending a bail 41 yards in a match at Brecon. Freakish it may have been, but it is a feat achievable only by a bowler of some speed. In September 1892 he took six for 41 at Llanelli who were bowled out for 83. But Llanelli then dismissed their opponents for just 33, much to the delight of *Spectator*, a cricket reporter with literary pretensions in the *Llanelli Mercury*, who wrote: 'This is no mean achievement. Llandovery has always been a thorn in the flesh and some of the oldest of the Llanelli XI who have mourned in sackcloth and ashes when defeated by Llandovery – crack Llandovery – so many times in the past, could hardly realise the fact and the Llandoveryites – well, they would they were "dreaming again".' He added: 'Llanelli had a professional called Briddon and facing the thunderbolts of C.P.Lewis, he made a very fine display.'

The following year, he turned out again for M.C.C. against Glamorgan at Swansea, and made a half-century in the visitors' total of 204. It took him only 18 minutes, with a six and ten 4s, all from one end, without receiving a ball from the other. Then he was run out. However, the match allowed him to rub shoulders once again with several leaders of the social and political world in South Wales – an increasingly important consideration as in 1894 he was elected Mayor of Llandovery.

Besides donning the mayoral chain, 1894 also saw Lewis give evidence at hearings held in the Town Hall, Llansawel to the Royal Commission on Land in Wales. His appearance related to claims raised by the tenants on the estate of his brother, David James Lewis, at Gilfach and Llwyn Celyn. They alleged that David had brought pressure to bear and compelled all of his tenants, including those who were nonconformist or chapel-attending, to go to church, otherwise they would be evicted. During his cross-examination before Lord Kenyon, the

Mr. C. P. Lewis, M.A., J.P.

Big fish in Llandovery pool.

chairman of the Commission's hearings, C.P. steadfastly refuted these claims. 'I know that my brother never brought any such influence to bear,' he told the inquiry, proving as he had done on the rugby and cricket fields that he was a man of principle and would firmly stand up for what he believed to be right, especially when the good name of the family might be tarnished by idle gossip.

Despite his duties of office, he still found plenty of time for cricket for the town club. His bowling was not always effective, though, and there were indications that Llandovery were slipping out of the top flight of South Wales clubs. In July, Swansea reached 225 for four at St. Helen's, despite C.P.'s bowling toil. Later that month, though, he had four for 19 as Llandovery bowled Llanelli out for 87. At the end of the month, in another match against Llanelli, he batted at number three and scored 27 out of 120 before taking six for 14. Three of the other wickets were taken by the Rev C.E.Chapman,[34] whose antics with the ball certainly caught the attention of a local journalist. The report suggests something of the 'serious but enjoyable' atmosphere of these games, all of course, 'non-League':

> I will describe the funny first. The fantastic bowling of C.E.Chapman was one of the funniest of the afternoon's proceedings. I shall not quickly forget the initial hop, the long run and the strong delivery. But it didn't end there. The genial reverend then comes racing up the pitch, looks in the batsman's eyes with the fierceness of a warrior, and ends up pirouetting round the wickets and taking a long walk into the outfield. I hadn't seen anything funnier on the cricket field for a long time and it caught on immensely. He roared his orders to the field and as the catches went wandering about his deep register could be heard giving instructions to the prospective catchees, 'Mind the twist' … 'More to the left' … 'Allow for the bounce'. And then, when the catch didn't come off, the same deep register exhausted itself in exclamations of disgust, 'Stupid boy' … 'Silly fellow' and 'Come away from there.' The Rev C.E.Chapman gave us good fun and did a great deal to enliven what otherwise would have been a very dull innings. The stand of C.P.Lewis and C.E.Chapman was one of the finest bits of batting in the match and I am sorry there were so few here to witness it.

In 1895 both C.P.Lewis and Douglas Jones accepted an invitation to join a Swansea and District eighteen to play the United South of England Eleven – the professional side still kept alive by county players who fancied some extra cash. The United South were mainly Surrey players. Tom Hayward, the England and Surrey bat, bowled Lewis once and Jones twice. Llandovery's rugby international Conway Rees and their professional Jenner also played. Lewis did not get any wickets. In June 1895, Lewis and Jones also took part in a two-day reunion match for the South Wales Cricket Club, in a side comprising many of C.P.'s generation of cricketers, against Glamorgan at St Helen's. Jones scored 95 in the first innings and Lewis 50 in the second, but they were seen off by nine wickets, through a 156 from Harold Letcher and ten

---

34   C.E.Chapman played five matches for Cambridge University in 1882 and 1883 without winning a Blue; he played two Minor Counties championship matches for Hertfordshire in 1895. Muscular Christianity, it will be noted, thrived yet.

wickets in the match by William Sweet-Escott.[35] Of Lewis'
contribution, the Press reported that 'the Champion Cricketer of
South Wales [hence the sub-title of this book] took his threes and
fours as plentifully as blackberries'. The following year, playing for
Llandovery against Swansea, Lewis scored 29 whilst batting at
number three, but got no wickets. Billy Bancroft – the son of C.P.'s
former coach, and Glamorgan's first homegrown professional –
went on to score 81 for Swansea. Against Llanelli, Lewis top-scored
with 26 out of 71 and took four for 16, but Llanelli still won by 34
runs.

A reunion.
The South Wales C.C. side which played Glamorgan at St. Helen's, Swansea in
June 1895. C.P. is sitting second from the right.

By 1897, our eccentric cleric Chapman and his brother Frank had
both left Llandovery. Lewis and D.T.M.Jones opened the batting
against Llanelli in May. In a return match he batted at number six
and scored 24 out of just 62 in another defeat. Against Swansea it
was 21 out of 63, though there were three wickets when he opened

---

35   It had been hoped that both W.G. and E.M.Grace would re-appear for their old
club but, on the day, neither appeared.

the bowling. Llanelli's Percy Rees, set to become Carmarthenshire's leading Minor Counties bat, was bowled by Lewis for 0 in 1898, in a match in which the declining Llandovery were all out for 22.

By the late 1890s, both the Llandovery Town side, as well as Lewis and Jones, were not the force they were, and the Town side suffered several heavy defeats, including one in 1898 when they were dismissed by Llanelli for just 22. Perhaps out of a feeling of loyalty to his home side, C.P. continued to turn out for the Llandovery Town eleven, although by 1900 he was scoring little at number seven and rarely took many wickets with his bowling which was nearer slow-medium, rather than medium-fast.[36] In 1902 and 1903 he was missing from the team, as civic and professional duties took their toll. Indeed, he was appointed Mayor of Llandovery again in 1904/05. Perhaps by now it was time for him to fade from the cricket scene, and to enjoy married life with Lizzie, together with their cook and maid in their home on the outskirts of Llandovery.

---

36   The 1901 Census records C.P., his wife Elizabeth and her sister Sarah in a house on the outskirts of Llandovery, not far from the College, with a 36-year-old cook and a maid, ten years younger. In 1911 his household still had two live-in domestic staff.

Chapter Eleven
County Cricket for Carmarthenshire

There was, though, to be a further twist to C.P.'s cricket tale.

When the South Wales Club broke up in 1888, it was with a recommendation that its leading lights go away and form individual county teams. Glamorgan were up and running almost immediately, and were soon followed by Monmouthshire. Questions were asked about forming a Carmarthenshire team, especially as there were many good cricketers in the county, with both Llandovery and Llanelli rated amongst the top rank of Welsh amateur clubs, with the likes of Swansea, Neath and Cardiff – a rating that can be seen mirrored in Welsh rugby clubs up until the dawn of professionalism in the 1990s.

There is no doubt the top players wanted county cricket, and their wish became more strident when the Minor Counties Championship started up in 1895. Such was the respect in which C.P.Lewis was held that every suggestion for a Carmarthenshire side being formed was deferred to him – and nothing ever happened. When Llanelli, for instance, held their annual general meeting in 1889, the minutes record that 'a discussion ensued as to county cricket and it was decided to ask Mr C.P.Lewis to take steps in the matter'. We can sympathise with the now middle-aged Lewis. He had his legal work – as a self-employed man he had to think of his practice and his clients expected him to give them priority, too – and his municipal duties as Mayor and later as a magistrate. Llandovery would of course have been much quieter than Llanelli, bustling with boom-town energy as tin and coal poured out of its port, making it one of the biggest industrial successes of the 1890s. The sporting ambitions were achieved by the town's famous rugby team, the 'Scarlet Runners', who became a major part of the growing success of Welsh rugby.

Many of the successful rugby players were good-class cricketers as well, with Frank Powell, a Llanelli centre and a decent middle-order bat joining Lewis when the old South Wales Club came back together, as we have seen, for a final swansong to play Glamorgan in a friendly at Swansea in 1895. As year followed year, Lewis was clearly content with social cricket, and others took the lead in organising county matches in Carmarthenshire.

In 1904 he could still top-score for Llandovery against Llanelli, and take good wickets, including that of Claude Warner, later of Glamorgan. In that same year, Llanelli tried to arrange a Carmarthenshire *v* Glamorgan match. J.H.Brain, the Glamorgan secretary, was keen, but in the end, he could not interest his amateurs – who were already involved in a substantial Minor County programme – to travel to West Wales for a two-day friendly. However, there was a trial match at Stradey Park, which was described by the local newspaper as being 'under the auspices of the county club'. Some sort of entity had clearly been created, but C.P. did not seem to be involved as he was noticeably absent amongst the 29 players who took part.

A similar match was arranged for 1906, but it had to be cancelled through 'cold and wet' in early April. A Carmarthenshire fixture was secured against the Gentlemen of Essex for whom Charlie McGahey, who had played Test cricket for England, scored 305 not out, the highest score at Stradey Park in any class of cricket. Lewis did not play, nor against the Gentlemen of Glamorgan or for an all-amateur side which played Shropshire.

Outgunned.
Carmarthenshire and the Gentlemen of Essex line up before their match at Llanelli on 9 and 10 July, 1906. C.P.McGahey (dark blazer and pads, sitting, and not a 'true' amateur) scored a triple century for the visitors.

In truth, the ageing Lewis was not amongst the best players in the county any more and, in the middle of his second term as Mayor, he clearly had other things on his mind. There was further evidence of his dwindling abilities in the match reports for his occasional appearances for Llandovery, such as the match against Llanelli in August 1906 when he struck 17 batting at number six, but according to the account, 'the veteran [was] slogging at the bowling'.

The following year, he agreed to help out the county organisation, besides agreeing to play alongside Douglas Jones for Carmarthenshire in their two-day match against Shropshire at the Llandovery Town ground. Only one innings was played on each side and neither did anything of note, but Lewis' presence amongst the county's officials was a major boost, as he was still regarded as one of the leading figures in sport in West Wales.

The proactive officials from Llanelli were delighted when he joined their county committee and helped them with their application to join the Minor Counties Championship. There were few other candidates with such excellent connections and, in the winter of 1907/08, their application was successful. By this time, the Minor Counties competition had been split into four regional divisions. Glamorgan had topped theirs, with Carmarthenshire being invited to join that division, as Dorset switched to the southern division.

The 'official' Minor Counties Championship was now in its fourteenth season and the new challenge seems to have appealed to C.P., who by then was 54 years old. Whilst his abilities as a bowler and batsman had largely deserted him, his appetite for the game remained keen – his desire for Carmarthenshire to do well was even sharper. Had it been Glamorgan or Monmouthshire who had called on his services, he probably would have swiftly declined the invitation, but with the pride of Carmarthenshire at stake, it was a completely different matter. The king of Llandovery cricket could not say no.

The first Minor Counties season began with a visit by Monmouthshire to Stradey Park. Lewis, though chairing the county committee, let the younger amateurs fill the team, with Llandovery and Llanelli – easily the strongest two clubs – providing the bulk of the starting eleven. Later in the season, enthusiasm started to wane, and some of the young thrusters had to go back to earning a living by the time the first home match was staged at the

Llandovery College ground on 10 and 11 August. With playing resources fully stretched, Lewis was drafted into the eleven. He duly scored 10 at number eight and didn't bowl in what proved to be a rain-affected contest, but the match might have taken more out of Lewis than the bare figures suggest: he didn't play for Llandovery against Llanelli a week later, probably because his body was still aching. *Wisden* pronounced on Carmarthenshire's season – they lost seven out of eight and drew one, without in that match securing a first innings lead – that they 'did not get on very well' and ascribed the poor outcome to an absence of professional bowlers.

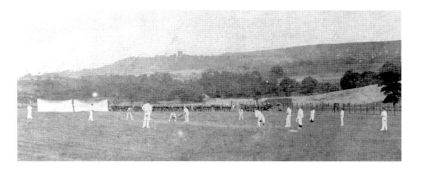

Play under way, despite static fielders,
in the Minor Counties championship match
between Glamorgan and Carmarthenshire at The Gnoll, Neath in June, 1908.

Tragedy struck in January 1909 when Lizzie died. Not for the first time in his life, he had to mourn and grieve the loss of someone who meant so much to him. Gradually, C.P. got over his tragic loss and perhaps the arrival of the 1909 season was something of a blessing. He started in the first match of the Minor County programme against Glamorgan at Stradey Park, making a crisp and unbeaten 33 coming in at number ten in the first innings – an effort which saw him subsequently promoted up to number seven for the second innings. However, he was caught off the clever spin bowling of Harry Creber for four as the game ended in a heavy defeat. There were many changes in the home side who, it was reported, 'gave the most wretched exhibition of fielding imaginable,' as Glamorgan rattled up 292, with Sweet-Escott scoring a fine 129 as his side comfortably won by an innings and 125 runs.

Lewis also played against Devon at Llandovery, but rain throughout the second day meant that he was not called upon to bat. When another player pulled out of the match against Cornwall at Camborne, Lewis stepped into the breach again and scored 21 and five on what was described as an easy-paced wicket. He also bowled three overs, but went for 25 runs as Cornwall found conditions, and the Welsh attack, very much to their liking as they posted 443. The Carmarthenshire side then travelled on to Torquay to meet Devon, but with Llanelli's Hugh Howell available for the match, Lewis stood down.

These were far from happy times for Carmarthenshire, who were rapidly establishing a reputation as all-time whipping boys of the Minor County competition. The county again finished last in the Western Division: out of eight matches, they lost five, all by an innings, and drew three, though this time they did have a first innings lead to report, against Cornwall. The qualification rules didn't help their cause either, as professionals had to be playing for the local clubs for two years before they could be selected for the county side. Consequently, Carmarthenshire missed the chance of using Sri Lankan Albert Holsinger, who was the professional with Llanelli in 1910, as well as, a year later, the South African googly bowler, Ernie Vogler. Lewis faced up to Holsinger on a wet wicket as Llandovery played Llanelli in May 1910. He lasted 15 minutes and scored five against a series of fast, sharply lifting deliveries from the Sinhalese bowler.

In 1910, Carmarthenshire continued with their Minor Counties campaign, this year to better effect. They won three games out of eight, beating Cornwall once and Dorset twice, all with Lewis present on the field of play. He batted at number nine when Cornwall visited Stradey Park in a match which saw Cornwall bowled out 29 in the second innings as Carmarthenshire gained one of their few wins. Against Dorset at Stradey a few weeks later he was bowled by Chester-Master for nought, but in the second knock he came in at 153 for nine and took the score to 213, scoring 28* and hitting four 4s as Carmarthenshire won again by 162 runs. Lewis appeared in the return contest at Poole Park the next week, won by four wickets, where he was promoted to number eight, before playing again against Cornwall in the following days.

In 1911, apparently now retired from his legal practice – the Census records his occupation as 'private means' – he captained a County Colts sixteen against Llanelli, batting as last man as he

C.P. in his last season with Carmarthenshire.

eyed up the coming talent and made a few recommendations about who seemed good enough to play in the Minor County games. In August he gave a glimpse of the past with a quixotic 46 against Monmouthshire at Abergavenny whilst batting at number nine. Together with Ernie Gee, a schoolmaster from Gowerton, he helped Carmarthenshire recover from 52 for seven, adding 73 with Gee and hitting out with glee, striking three 6s, two 4s and a 5, with all the sixes coming off the bowling of Arthur Silverlock, one of the great stalwarts of Minor Counties cricket. His swash-buckling innings however could not prevent Monmouthshire from inflicting a 133-run defeat.

He played against Buckinghamshire at Slough, opening the batting with little success when Carmarthenshire followed on and also in the return match at Llanelli, when 'the veteran suffered an injury to the leg', though he scored 30 at number ten with four 4s and two 3s. Against Berkshire he played in a most dramatic contest at the Stradey Park ground when his shooting skills were nearly required as the Berkshire team had to be escorted to the town's railway station in their horse-drawn brakes by riflemen. In fact, they got the last train out of Llanelli before the great 1911 Railway Strike saw trains grind to a halt.

The match, played on 4 and 5 August, is down in the scorebook as 'abandoned owing to rain', but that may be a fiction or a hasty misspelling of 'train'. E.H.D.Sewell, the Essex amateur who became a prolific cricket journalist, was with the team and described events in the town known as 'Tinopolis' as 'too hot'. Llanelli was seething with unrest as strikers and their supporters blocked the level crossings either side of the town's station. The Home Secretary (Winston Churchill) and the Government sent in troops, the Riot Act was read, the Army opened fire and killed two, after which the rolling-stock containing their kit and ammunition was set on fire, whilst shops and offices associated with the local magistrates were burned down. With all of this going on around them, the cricketers of Berkshire knew they were in the wrong place, and they wisely headed out of the Carmarthenshire town.[37] Soon after, although they did return to Llanelli for one last match, on 16 and 17 August, Carmarthenshire's brief sojourn in the Minor Counties Championship came to an end, with the drama in Llanelli in early August overshadowing their lacklustre cricket.

In the season as a whole they had played eight matches, and had lost seven, with *Wisden* commenting that 'they fell away badly' and were 'a poor team all round'. They pulled out that year, and though they played a few friendly matches up to 1920, have never returned to the Minor Counties competition as an independent entity. In four seasons in the competition, they had played thirty-two games, winning three and losing 26. In three drawn games, they had first innings lead in just one; and of the 26 matches lost, 17 were by an innings. In championship matches they had scored their runs at an average of 14.30 per wicket, but had conceded them at more than twice that rate, at 30.60.[38] Numbers were against them in another way, too. With a resident population of around 140,000, smaller than almost all the other counties in the competition, it was not surprising that Carmarthenshire did not have the playing or financial resources to sustain a side capable of taking on their competitors on credible terms. So it had been a noble enterprise, and no doubt C.P. drew some pride from the fact that he played a part in all three of their winning matches.[39]

The following summer, Lewis was able to smile as he remarried and wed Jane ('Jennie') Bentley. That year Lewis again played and oversaw the Carmarthenshire Colts against Llanelli, in addition to batting at number eight for Carmarthenshire in a friendly against Glamorgan. He reached 56 against Monmouthshire in a high-scoring draw at Llandovery, obtaining his runs 'in a carefree manner'. As the scorebook shows – 4 4 4 4 4 4 1 1 4 2 1 4 2 4 4 2 1 1 4 1 – it was full of lusty and violent blows in what proved to be his last major innings against decent opposition.

---

37   Our particular thanks to local historian John Edwards, son-in-law of Dai Davies, for this information.

38   Carmarthenshire scored 250 in an innings three times in four seasons; their opponents reached this figure 23 times.

39   He may though have been embarrassed as a retired solicitor that he could not guarantee opponents safe passage in his county!

In his element. Lewis, at the centre of this photograph, is very much the senior man here.
The match is Carmarthenshire v Ammanford, at Llandovery in 1911.
Standing (l to r): O.D.Edwards, C.S.Trubshaw, A.R.Trubshaw, W.Davies, J.Southern, W.J.Bancroft, G.Owen, J.Maxwell, R.Brunt, Dr.Morgan, not known, Dr Evans, R.Seymour, I.Evans.
Seated: J.E.Morgan, J.T.Davies, Isaac Evans, P.Cook, C.P.Lewis, W.T.Price, B.P.Rees, H.Howell, H.Jones, G.M.Jeffreys.
On the ground: G.W.Davies and W.N.Thomas (umpires), D.P.Rees and H.Edmunds (scorers).

Chapter Twelve
Later Years

The outbreak of the Great War brought an abrupt, but not overdue, end to C.P.'s playing career. The world was very different when cricket resumed in 1919, with David Hughes-Morgan taking over as captain of the Llandovery Town side. Like Lewis, Hughes-Morgan had been educated at Oxford, but there the similarity ceased as the new captain had a plethora of other sporting interests, including participating in hill-climbs in a big black Mercedes, sailing with the Swansea Bay and Bristol Channel yacht clubs, and in the winter months hunting and horse-racing, serving as a director of Chepstow Racecourse. He was still able to call on the services, albeit for a couple of years only, of Douglas Jones, whilst C.P. maintained his involvement through umpiring and serving on the committee of both the Town club and the Carmarthenshire county side.

From 1900, C.P. and Jennie lived in Llandovery at Llandingat House, described as 'a two-storeyed house crowned with a galaxy of seventeen chimney pots'. When he moved there is unclear, as there was a Mr.Harries in residence up until 1899. His was a comfortable life as a country solicitor. He and his fellow professional men worked in a seemingly unchanging era of varnished oak and strong-smelling leather, seated behind giant desks. Whiffs of Edwardian Llandovery still survive to this day. From 1899 Lewis served as a magistrate in the courtroom on stilts above Llandovery's open air market hall. It closed, unchanged, only in the early years of the twenty-first century – atop a winding staircase with wooden treads worn down by myriads of feet; a narrow wooden bench towering above the sunken centre floor with a four sided dock crowned by metal railings, more decoration than bars; and a series of box like structures with wooden seats for the various solicitors and court petitioners.

Llandovery's Black Ox Bank was equally unchanging, despite being taken over by Lloyd's in the twentieth century. It was here in the 1990s that Llandovery C.C. found that they owned a musty deposit box left behind by C.P.Lewis. No monetary riches were inside, but instead historical affluence. The 1890s scorebook, a big leather-bound ledger in copperplate clerk's handwriting, not only recording matches ball-by-ball, but each with a handwritten match report. Also there was the Carmarthenshire scorebook from the second half of the Minor County years, and Lewis' Carmarthenshire caps, with their gaudy circles of many colours, plus the regal orange and purple of the South Wales Club.

The Carmarthenshire book is less impressive than the Llandovery one. It is a ledger of Stephens-ink blue, embossed, at first sight, with the unlikely legend 'E.C.B. Cricket Scoring Book', but on closer examination the initials are identifiable as G.C.B. – Geo.C. Bussey, the cricket supplier. It carries the written legend 'Minor Counties Scoring Book – Carmarthenshire County, 1.8.1910 to 5.8.1920', though the last few years are friendlies. Tucked in the first page is a postcard with a written 'Order of Going In' for one of the later matches. Sadly, there is no place for the scorer's name, but, as C.P.Lewis did everything else, we can be sure he also did his spell in the box.

Lewis, as a country solicitor of that age, was meticulous in filing things away. David Smith, uncle of England's Ed Smith, found more of his effects, including a lengthy will. 'One gets the strong impression that he drafted his own meticulous will, with its lament on the cost of living after the Great War,' Smith wrote. 'There on pages 3 and 4 appears "I give and bequeath to my said Trustees the South Wales Cricket silver Challenge Cup presented to me by the old South Wales Cricket Club upon its dissolution in 1886 ... upon trust that my Trustees shall permit the said ... to be used and enjoyed by my said great nephew Meryn Lewis during his life."' Meryn, also a lawyer, passed it to his nephew in about 1965. The cup had been kept in a wooden box for many years and was still in excellent condition. In 1983, as Llandovery College played the XL Club it was handed back to the College, to be displayed with their other cricketing heirlooms like the bails from the 1956 Test when Jim Laker took all ten wickets in an innings; presented by the match umpire Emrys Davies – the former Glamorgan all-rounder – who had sent his son Peter to Llandovery.

Even when well into his sixties, C.P. still travelled up to London to watch cricket at Lord's and rugby at Twickenham, but in the autumn of 1922, he was taken ill whilst watching the Varsity match. Sadly, he never fully recovered and he died peacefully at his home in Llandovery on Monday, 28 May 1923, months short of his 'three score years and ten'.

Just two days before, J.T.D.Llewelyn had celebrated his 87th birthday. Lewis was not well enough to attend the party held by the Grand Old Man of Welsh sport who was deeply moved by the death of the man who some fifty years before had been his right-hand man with the South Wales Club and had spent so much time promoting both cricket and rugby in Wales. By the time of his passing, both games were in a healthy state, with Glamorgan having achieved, in 1921, the goal that the South Wales Cricket Club had hoped for by being elevated into the County Championship. C.P.Lewis lived long enough to see Glamorgan achieve first-class status, and perhaps there was a smile on his face when he read in the newspapers that their inaugural side in the County Championship – they beat Sussex at Cardiff Arms Park – included a descendant of the Whittingtons of Neath, who had instilled a love of ball games when he first entered Llandovery College.

C.P. left an estate worth £18,933 (equivalent to £750,000 at 2009 prices) and his funeral was attended by the great and the good of Welsh sporting circles. Many warm tributes were paid to this great Welsh sporting pioneer and a man who held dear the true Corinthian values of sporting participation. Perhaps the last word on Lewis should go to his former Llandovery teammate Frank Chapman, who was living in Wokingham when Lewis died. Despite having moved away from South Wales he was sufficiently moved to write to *The Cricketer* magazine, saying C.P. was

> one of the most enthusiastic cricketers I ever met. He never missed the Varsity match and Gentlemen v Players. In fact he spent his honeymoon at Lord's – a true sporting gentleman!

Acknowledgements

The authors would like to thank Ian Hunt, the Warden of Llandovery College for his foreword, and the following for their assistance and encouragement: Tim Auty, Philip Bailey, Katrina Coopey, Howard Evans, Christopher Jeens, John Jenkins, Bryn Jones, Roger Mann, Tom Marks, Duncan Pierce, Gwyn Prescott, David Smith, J.Hugh Thomas, and Prof Gareth Williams. Various members of Llandovery Town and Llanelli Cricket Clubs have helped us, as have Llandovery and Llandeilo Rugby Clubs: our thanks to them all.

We have received much-appreciated professional assistance from archivists at King's School, Gloucester; Llandovery College; Christ College, Brecon; and Jesus College Oxford, as well as from the staff at Gloucester Library; The Guildhall Library, London; Llandovery Magistrates' Court; Llanelli Public Library; the Oxfordshire Local Studies Library; and Swansea Library.

Many thanks to David Jeater for his editorial work; to Kit Bartlett and Gerald Hudd for their assistance with proof-reading; as well as to Zahra Ridge and Peter Griffiths for their sterling work in the design, typesetting and production of this volume.

Bibliography

Books and articles

H.S.Altham and E.W.Swanton, *A History of Cricket* [Third Edition], George Allen and Unwin, 1947

Don Ambrose, *The Cricket Season of 1876: A Statistical Survey*, ACS Publications, 2000

Philip Bailey, Philip Thorn and Peter Wynne-Thomas, *Who's Who of Cricketers* [Second Edition], Hamlyn in association with ACS, 1993

C.J.Bartlett, First-Class Cricket and the Church, in *Journal of the Cricket Society*, Vols 11 and 12, 1983-1985

John Billot, *History of Welsh International Rugby,* Roman Way Books, 1999

D.E.Davies, *Cardiff Rugby Club 1876–1975: One Hundred Years at Cardiff Arms Park*, Starling Press Ltd, 1976

John Edwards, *Remembrance of a Riot*, Llanelli Borough Council, 1989

W.Gareth Evans, *A History of Llandovery College*, Trustees of Llandovery College, 1981

David Farmer, *The All Whites: The Life and Times of Swansea RFC*, DFPS Ltd, 1995

Bill Frindall, *The Wisden Book of Cricket Records* [Fourth Edition], Headline, 1998

Donald E.Hall (ed), *Muscular Christianity: Embodying the Victorian Age*, Cambridge University Press, 1994

Bob Harragan, *Criced: A History of Cricket in Wales from the Beginnings to 1900*, privately published, 1980

Bob Harragan, *Some Records of the Carmarthenshire County Cricket Club*, privately published, 2000

Andrew Hignell, *A Favorit Game: Cricket in South Wales before 1914* , University of Wales Press, 1992

Andrew Hignell, *A Who's Who of Glamorgan County Cricket Club: 1888–1991*, Breedon Books, 1992

Andrew Hignell, *Cricket in Wales: An Illustrated History*, University of Wales Press, 2008

Gareth Hughes, *One Hundred Years of Scarlet*, Llanelli Rugby Football Club, 1983

R.Brinley Jones, *Floreat Landubriense*, Trustees of Llandovery
College, 1998

P.E.Reynolds, *The Australian Cricketers' Tour Through Australia,
New Zealand and Great Britain in 1878*, J.W.McKenzie, 1980

D.T. and J.B.Smith, *South Wales Cricket Club, 1859–1886*,
privately published, 1989

David Smith, T.B.Jones, in *Journal of the Cricket Society*, Vol 7,
1975, pp 61-62

David Smith and Gareth Williams, *Fields of Praise: The Official
History of the Welsh Rugby Union*, University of Wales Press,
1980

Wray Vamplew, *Play up and Play the Game*, Cambridge
University Press, 1988

J.R.Webber, *The Chronicle of W.G.*, ACS Publications, 1998

Regular publications and newspapers
The Cambrian newspaper
Cambrian News
Carmarthen Journal newspaper
Cricket magazine
The Cricketer magazine
Gloucester Journal
James Lillywhite's Cricketers' Annual
John Lillywhite's Cricketers' Companion
Llanelly and County Guardian
Oxford and Cambridge Undergraduates' Journal
South Wales Daily News
The Times
Western Mail
The Welshman newspaper
Wisden's Cricketers' Almanack

Websites
www.cricketarchive.com, www.mswth.com, yba.llgc.org.uk

Appendix
Some Statistics

(a) First-Class cricket for Oxford University, 1876

Batting and Fielding

M	I	NO	R	HS	Ave	100	50	Ct
5	7	0	76	33	10.85	-	-	2

Notes: Lewis' highest first-class score was 33 in the University's first innings v Gentlemen of England at Magdalen College Ground, Oxford. Six of his seven dismissals were caught.

Bowling

O	M	R	W	BB	Ave	5i
283.1	98	501	17	7-35	29.47	1

Notes: Overs were of four balls in 1876. Lewis' only five-wicket return in first-class cricket was 7 for 35, off 36.3 overs in M.C.C.'s second innings at Magdalen College Ground, Oxford. In all first-class matches, nine of his wickets were bowled and eight caught, including one caught-and-bowled and one caught by the wicket-keeper. He took wickets at the rate of one per 66.6 balls and conceded runs at a rate equivalent to 2.65 runs per six-ball over.

(b) South Wales Club representative matches, 1874-1895

Full scorecards are not available for all the matches in which Lewis made appearance for the South Wales, but the figures below give an indication of Lewis' achievements at the height of his powers.

Batting and Fielding

M	I	NO	R	HS	Ave	100	50	Ct
50	82	3	1696	120	21.46	1	8	42

Notes: Lewis' highest score for South Wales was 120 against Surrey Club and Ground at The Oval in 1876.

Bowling

Balls	M	R	W	BB	Ave	5i	10m
5902	505	2551	214	9-39	11.92	18	5

Notes: Overs were of four balls until the end of 1889 season, and from then on during his South Wales career, of five balls. His best innings return for the club was nine for 39 against Clifton, in their second innings, at Cardiff Arms Park in 1882. Overall he took his wickets at the rate of one per 27.5 balls and conceded runs at a rate equivalent to 2.59 per six-ball over.

(c) Minor Counties cricket for Carmarthenshire, 1908-1911

Batting and Fielding

M	I	NO	R	HS	Ave	100	50	Ct
19	33	4	316	46	10.89	-	-	5

Note: Lewis' highest score in Minor Counties cricket was 46 in Carmarthenshire's second innings against Monmouthshire at Abergavenny in 1911, when he was 57 years old.

Bowling

O	M	R	W	BB	Ave	5i
3	0	25	0	0-25	-	-

Notes: Lewis bowled in only one Minor Counties match, against Cornwall in their only innings at Camborne in 1909. Overs were of six balls at that time.

Index

A page number in bold type indicates an illustration.